INTERNATIO

CATHOLIC

INTERNATIONAL RELATIONS

FROM A

CATHOLIC STANDPOINT

TRANSLATED FROM THE FRENCH

Delos, J. T.

Edited for the Catholic Union of
International Studies (Irish Section)

BY

STEPHEN J. BROWN, S.J.

BROWNE AND NOLAN LIMITED

DUBLIN   BELFAST   CORK   WATERFORD
LONDON: 18 RED LION PASSAGE, HOLBORN, W.C.1

1932

De licentia Sup. Ord.

LAURENTIUS J. KIERAN, S.J.,
Praep. Prov. Hib.

Dublini, die 2° Maii, anno 1932.

Nihil Obstat: JOANNES KELLY,
                       Censor Theol. Dep.

Imprimi potest: ✠ EDUARDUS,
                       Archiep. Dublinen.,
                       Hiberniae Primas.

Dublini, die 30° Aprilis, anno 1932.

Made and Printed in Ireland by Browne and Nolan Ltd., Dublin.

FOREWORD TO THE ENGLISH TRANSLATION

THE little book of which this is a translation appeared in France under the title *La Société Internationale*. We have chosen for the English version a title which seems to express the nature of its contents in a way that will be clearer to the public for which it is intended. The origin of the work and the objects at which it aims are clearly set forth by Mgr. Beaupin in his Introduction. All that need be said here concerns the present translation.

It was undertaken by the Irish Section of the Catholic Union of International Studies, with the kind permission of Mgr. Beaupin and of the publishers, to whom our best thanks are hereby tendered. Part I. has been translated by the Rev. M. Langford, Dean of Residence, University College, Dublin, Part II. by Miss Pauline Delany, Parts III. and IV. by the Editor, while the translator of Mgr. Beaupin's Preface prefers to remain anonymous. Mr. Albert Le Brocquy has revised the figures and other data in Part III.

It is hoped that the little work, in its English dress, will prove useful to further the objects for which the Catholic Union exists, viz., the serious study of international affairs in the light of Catholic doctrine and with the aid of Catholic principles. The very word "international" tends to make us think of such studies as something remote from the daily lives and ordinary concerns of individual citizens. But when we call to mind on the one hand that the success or failure of such international organisations as the League of Nations and the International Labour Office, and of such international movements as the movements for peace and disarmament, depends very largely on the state of public opinion—that public opinion being itself the resultant of many individual opinions; and on the other hand that friendship or hatred between nations arises out of a national temper, made up of the prejudices, antagonisms, and fancies of many individuals, it is not hard to realize that such studies may have a very practical bearing. Moreover, the relations between nation and nation are largely governed by the attitude of their respective citizens towards their own nation and its government. National movements have their repercussion in the international sphere. What the Hitlerite is thinking about Germany is a matter of concern to all Germany's neighbours, and therefore to the world at large. One cannot study internationalism without studying nationalism, patriotism, and anti-patriotism. And such matters, however little one may realize it, are the concern of everybody.

To enhance whatever usefulness this little book may have, a short list of books, chiefly in English, for further study, has been added.

THE EDITOR.

February 9, 1932.

SOME BOOKS FOR FURTHER STUDY

WE may mention in the first place two works brought out by the Catholic Union of International Studies (Fribourg) since *La Société Internationale* was published viz. :—

Les grands Problèmes internationaux de l'heure présente. (Paris : Editions Spes.) 1930.

La Pensée catholique dans le monde contemporain. (Paris : Editions Spes.) 1931.

These books consist principally of lectures delivered at the International Catholic Weeks held at Geneva in 1929 and 1930. An Irish viewpoint is set forth in :

Ireland and the League of Nations, by Bolton C. Waller. (Dublin : The Talbot Press.) 1925.

There is no need to give an extended list of general works on the League of Nations. Several lists have been issued by the National Book Council, 3 Henrietta Street, Covent Garden, W.C. 2, and may be had for a few pence. The output of the League of Nations itself is enormous. Lists of its publications may easily be obtained from the Secretariat at Geneva.

Useful surveys are :

Ten Years' Life of the League of Nations, compiled by John Eppstein (of the Catholic Council of International Relations). (London : The Mayfair Press.) 1929 ; and

Ten Years of World Co-Operation, issued officially by the Secretariat of the League. The Foreword is by the Secretary of the League, Sir Eric Drummond, a Catholic.

The Secretariat of the League publishes an official handbook, under the title *The Aims and Organisation of the League of Nations.* It is very well done and quite inexpensive.

The League of Nations from Idea to Reality. Its place in history and in the world of to-day. By Robert Jones and S. S. Sherman (London : Pitman, 1929), with its maps and photographs and diagrams is very useful for use in class or lecture hall.

Finally, I venture to mention a delightful book of an entirely different type from any of the above—*L'esprit de Genève,* by Robert de Traz. (Paris : Grasset.) 1929.

Concord is a little monthly review published by the League of Nations Society of Ireland. It is " non-sectarian " but respectful towards Catholic teaching.

The remaining books on this list deal with international matters from the Catholic standpoint :—

Catholics and the Problem of Peace. By Joseph Keating, S.J. (Oxford : The Catholic Social Guild.) 1925.

A Primer of Peace and War. By Charles Plater, S.J. (Same Publishers.)

The Catholic Citizen : His National and International Responsibilities. Edited by John Eppstein. (London : Catholic Truth Society.)

Catholics and the League of Nations. By G. Elliot Anstruther. (Same Publishers.) 8 pages.

L'Organisation internationale du monde contemporain et la Papauté souveraine. Three Volumes. By Yves de la Brière, S.J. (Paris : Editions Spes.) 1926, 1927, 1930.

La Société Internationale. Edited by Mgr. Beaupin. (Paris : J. de Gigord.) 1928.

Bulletin Catholique Internationale. Directed by Maurice Vaussard (1 Rue de Fleurus, Paris VIᵉ). Monthly.

The Catholic Union of International Study : Its Organisation, Prospects, Results. A pamphlet of 12 pages, published at the Head Office of the Organisation, Fribourg, Switzerland. 1926.

Catholics and the League of Nations. By Stephen J. Brown. S.J. (Dublin : League of Nations Society of Ireland). 2d. 1929.

The Church and War. By Franziskus Stratmann, O.P. (London : Sheed and Ward.) 1930.

Paix et Guerre. (" La Vie Intellectuelle," Les Documents, February, 1932).

Patriotisme et Internationalisme—Société des Nations. By the Abbé Paulin Giloteaux. (Paris : Téqui.) 1931.

La Papauté et les Questions internationales. (Paris : Bloud et Gay.) 1931. Being a course of lectures delivered under the auspices of the Institut Pie XI.

The Catholic Council of International Relations (England) publishes a bulletin entitled *A Catholic Survey* (74 Victoria Street, London, S.W.).

The most ample and exhaustive discussion of international problems from the Catholic standpoint that has yet appeared is the report of the eighteenth " Semaine Sociale " of the French

Catholics, published in 1926; under the title *Le Problème de la Vie internationale*. (Paris : Gabalda.) It forms a volume of 726 pages. Among those who contributed papers were M. Eugène Duthoit, Louis le Fur, Père Desbuquois, S.J., Pères Rutten and Gillet, O.P., the Abbé Thellier de Poncheville, Max Turmann, Maurice Vaussard, and Mgr. Beaupin.

One of the best short accounts of the League is a pamphlet by Père Yves de la Brière, S.J., entitled *La Société des Nations, structure, fonctionnement, étude du texte constitutif*, published at Lyons by the " Chronique Sociale de France."

Another excellent popular account is *La Société des Nations*, by Père Dalmace Saget, O.P. (Liége : La Penséé Catholique.) 1931.

Just published (April 15, 1932). *Opinions Catholiques sur la limitation et la réduction des armements*, published for the Union Catholique d'Etudes Internationales by the Editions du Cerf, Juvisy, Seine-et-Oise.

CONTENTS

	PAGE
FOREWORD TO TRANSLATION. *By the Editor*	v
LIST OF BOOKS FOR FURTHER STUDY	ix
INTRODUCTION. *By Mgr. Beaupin*	1

PART I.

(*Translated by Rev. M. Langford, M.A.*)

CHRISTIAN PRINCIPLES AND INTERNATIONAL
RELATIONS. *By Père Delos, O.P.*

CHAPTER I.—THE NATIONS AND UNIVERSAL HUMAN
SOCIETY 13
    1. Man as a Social Being. 13
    2. Nation and Fatherland 15
    3. The Function of the Nation 18
    4. False Conceptions of Nationalism 21
    5. International Relations 26

CHAPTER II.—STATES AND THEIR JURIDICAL RELATIONS ... 31
    1. States as Moral Persons and Subject to Law 31
    2. Moral Laws Governing Inter-state Relations ... 34

CHAPTER III.—INTERNATIONAL SOCIETY 42
    1. The Basis of International Society 43
    2. The Principle of Order in International Society.
      Obligations of States 47

CHAPTER IV.—PEACE 53

CHAPTER V.—WAR 58
    1. Nature of War 58
    2. Conditions of just Warfare 60
    3. Treaties of Peace 68

PART II.

(Translated by Miss Pauline Delany)

THE WORK OF THE CATHOLIC CHURCH FOR PEACE.

By Canon Leman.

		PAGE
CHAPTER I.—EARLY CHRISTIAN TIMES	..	73
,, II.—THE BARBARIAN INVASIONS AND THE MEROVINGIAN PERIOD	..	76
,, III.—THE FEUDAL PERIOD ..	..	79
1. The Protection of the Weak and the " Peace of God "	..	82
2. The " Truce of God "	..	88
3. Chivalry and the Military Orders	..	91
4. The Third Order of St. Francis	..	94
5. Catholic Teaching on Peace and War	..	96
CHAPTER IV.—THE WORK OF THE POPES FOR PEACE IN THE MIDDLE AGES	..	99
1. Holy Wars	..	99
2. Arbitration and Pontifical Mediation	..	104
CHAPTER V.—MODERN TIMES	..	112
1. From the Renaissance to the Treaties of Westphalia	..	112
2. From the Treaties of Westphalia to the Beginning of the Nineteenth Century	..	121
CHAPTER VI.—THE ACTIVITIES OF THE PAPACY IN THE NINETEENTH AND TWENTIETH CENTURIES	..	124

PART III.

(Translated by the Editor)

ORGANISATION AND ACTIVITY OF THE LEAGUE OF NATIONS.

By M. Marcel Prelot.

I.—INTRODUCTORY	..	137
II.—ORGANISATION OF THE LEAGUE ..	..	139
III.—ACTIVITES OF THE LEAGUE	..	153
IV.—THE LEAGUE AND THE MAINTENANCE OF PEACE ..		162

PART IV.

(Translated by the Editor.)

THE INTERNATIONAL ORGANISATION OF LABOUR.

By M. Joseph Danel.

PAGE

CHAPTER   I.—THE REASONS FOR ITS CREATION   .. 173

    „   II.—HISTORICAL PRECEDENTS   175

    „   III.—THE TREATY OF VERSAILLES. SOME
            PRINCIPLES 178

    „   IV.—THE ORGANISATIONS SET UP BY THE
            TREATY   186

    „   V.—THE CARRYING OUT OF THE PLAN   .. 192

    „   VI.—PRACTICAL RESULTS   194

APPENDIX.—THE CATHOLIC UNION OF INTERNATIONAL
   STUDIES (IRISH SECTION). PROGRAMME OF STUDIES .. 197

INTRODUCTION

FOR nearly eight years the work of setting up institutions calculated to safeguard International Peace has been going on. While working to organise these institutions the various Governments have turned to educationalists urging them to work for the pacification of men's minds, asking them to teach the youth of the Nation their international duties, and to instruct them how to carry out these duties.

This desire for peace has found its practical expression in the efforts of the League of Nations to make itself and its ideals better known. As early as 1921, the League founded the Committee of Intellectual Co-operation, which, after extensive investigations, formulated the proposal that there should be official public instruction on the aims, means, and results attained by the institution functioning at Geneva. In 1925 it had already become clear that a body of pacifist Pedagogics was in process of elaboration, and that from experiments made it had been possible to draw conclusions useful to teachers, and worthy of being embodied in educational programmes.

From this sprang, in 1927, a booklet, one of the Geneva series, called : *How to Make the League of Nations Known and How to Develop the Spirit of Intellectual Co-operation.* Besides the points recommended to its members by the League, there will be found in it the measures already taken by various Governments to answer its appeal.   In it are to be found, as regards France, eight circulars issued by successive Ministers of Education to Education authorities setting before them in detail the points to be introduced into the Programmes, and the steps to be taken to spread the teaching contained in them.

The earliest of these documents, dated 18th August, 1921, and signed by M. Léon Bérard, orders the idea of the League to be placed on the Programmes of civic instruction in the higher Primary Schools (second year) as well as in the Programme of Normal Schools (second year : Political Sociology ; third year : History). A little later, 3rd December, 1923, the new Programmes for Secondary teaching were published.   In these are to be found for the class of Philosophy items bearing on the League of Nations, and on International relations.

Besides, almost yearly, on the eve of Armistice Day, November 11th, the Minister of Education sends a circular to the Staffs of Primary and Secondary Schools, asking them not merely to laud the heroism of those who fell in the war, but to bring out the efforts of their country, either at Geneva or elsewhere, to maintain world Peace, and to co-operate whole-heartedly in the work of the League.

Thus it became a question for French educationalists, in what way and to what extent they are to join in the efforts called for by the League. In France this is still a moot question. " Pacifist " Education, if given bluntly, and without qualification, can hurt not only lawful and sane patriotism, but even the Faith itself, as, on the other hand, it may seem, if imparted properly, quite in accord with love of country, and with the demands of the strictest orthodoxy. On the other hand, the League of Nations is a fact which cannot be ignored : and there exists a philosophic body of teaching on the duties and rights between nations. Finally, before long all these vexed questions will probably be a matter for investigation.

For all these reasons the Catholic Union of International Studies, a private association founded in 1920, numbering now adherents in some 20 countries, decided on this little book at its meeting in 1926. It entrusted its drawing-up to its own Committee of Intellectual Cooperation.

This Catholic Committee, which has followed day by day the work of Geneva, and has even taken its share in it, agreed with the French group of the Union to ask four Professors of the Catholic University of Lille, who were members of the French group, to write the work.

The Association of Establishments of Christian Education, to which are affiliated more than 600 colleges of Secondary Education either in France or in French-speaking countries, could not be indifferent to the situation described above. The book was submitted in manuscript to the President of this Association, Canon Guillemant, Vicar General of Arras, who gave it his approbation. Finally it was accepted by the publisher of the Association, M. de Gigord, to whom we owe deep gratitude for his ready help.

That is the history of the little volume. It remains for us to explain for whom it is intended. We offer it to Catholic Professors and Teachers, as well as to all who in post-college unions and study circles are in touch with the young; to the older boys in our Colleges and Schools. They will find in it ideas, briefly put, of course, but sufficient (hitherto only to be found in learned tomes or scattered in countless reviews) on the following subjects : the Church's teaching on the relations between Nations; the action of the Church in favour of international peace, either in the course of the world's history, or in our own day; the League of Nations as it actually exists; and on one of the most important creations of the Treaty of Versailles, namely the International Labour Organisation.

The intention has been, therefore, to put into their hands documents on which they can rely, to which they can turn in case of need without wasting time and study in a lengthy search. We have tried, therefore, on these delicate questions, to supply accurate data, thanks to which they will always be able to speak about peace without saying a word to hurt patriotism, and to speak on the

subject of the League of Nations without
belittling it or belauding it, but with precise
knowledge of the facts of the case.

This book is, therefore, no piece of propaganda for the League of Nations ; it is rather
an attempt to show it in its proper
light as one of the efforts of man to found
between nations a relationship based on
right and justice. In the first part Father
Delos shows how these efforts respond to the
deepest needs of man's nature especially in
our day. In the second, Canon Leman
appeals to History to show that the Catholic
Church, far from being uninterested in the
cause of peace, has always furthered it, either
by those movements she has set in motion,
or by the teaching she has ever given, and
continues to give, to her children, and to the
responsible heads of States. Lastly, M.
Prélot and M. Danel describe the International
Organisations of to-day, stressing as they go
along the real spirit of Christianity really
embodied in them though at times quite
unknown to the promotors. This they do
by showing their conformity on many points
with the teachings of Leo XIII. and
Benedict XV.

Thus the book is of wider scope than the

League of Nations as it exists to-day. The greater in its larger framework includes the less. Hence its use is clear. To impress on the young the spirit of International Co-operation professors and educators have only to appeal to what is sanest in philosophy, and to the History of the Church. They need only to emphasise this point of view when occasion offers—and the occasion will crop up at every hand's turn—in their daily lectures. They will by so doing prevent a false view of the past or a distorted view of the present from taking possession of their pupils' minds. They will warn them against the harm that threatens the virtue of Patriotism, when it is forced into the mould of pagan nationalism, as well as against the dangers to which internationalism is exposed when it takes the shape of a vague humanitarianism or when, as is the case in Russia to-day, it is made the tool of a propaganda aiming at the overthrow of the entire social order.

A moral rule is necessary for both patriotism and internationalism. This rule depends in its turn on belief in God, creator and lawgiver of mankind and of the world. These are postulates of right reason, but they are

confirmed and strengthened and ennobled by
Catholic Faith. This is, finally, the reason
why Christian teaching works not merely
for itself, but in defence of the elementary
principles of Natural Law, when it refuses
to accept those half explanations with which,
too often, certain minds are content.

By her universal character the Catholic
Church has ever been and still is a unique
teacher of International Co-operation. Among
her children in every domain of action,
natural or supernatural, everything is done
by co-ordination and co-operation. Yet this
does not in any way interfere with racial or
national genius in the peoples she gathers
to her, and binds together by baptism.
Rather is the richness and fruitfulness of her
influence the outcome of such national
contributions. It is in their emulation that
she finds the secret of her eternal youth.

Is not the hour come for Christian
educators to proclaim this with insistence,
giving proofs for the faith that is in them, at
a time when this spirit of co-operation, which
is being preached on all sides, is in danger of
remaining sterile because it is not based on
sound philosophy nor on any sound theory
of History which might explain whence it

comes and whence it has derived its power. But this is unduly solemn, you will say, for a preface to such a slender volume. But we have great hopes, and we should not have put them entirely into words, did we not say, that the authors of this book have striven to give voice to the recent teachings of Pius XI. who from his first Encyclical, *Ubi Arcano Dei*, published on 23rd December, 1923, made himself the Evangelist among the nations of " the Peace of Christ in the Kingship of Christ."

That peace, " daughter of Love, dwelling in the depths of the soul " we hope to prepare and promote by Christian Education. We hope to make known its holy demands, to search out in temporal institutions everything that is calculated to promote it, to remove from these institutions everything that would endanger its existence or prevent its growth. We must take these institutions as they are, and strive to make them what they ought to be. On the other hand, it must not be said that the Catholic teaching in France (a country whose patriotism has proved itself, whose devotion to the Church is so evident to all) has failed to cultivate in the souls confided to it a love of France entirely in

harmony with a love of peace. We are
striving to train Catholics who will be as
loyal citizens of the National as of the International Society; for it is by the right
fulfilment of our duties towards the former
that we shall best serve the latter.

MGR. BEAUPIN,

*President of the Committee on Intellectual
Co-operation of the Catholic Union for
International Studies.*

PART I

CHRISTIAN PRINCIPLES AND INTERNATIONAL RELATIONS

By Père Delos, o.p.

CHAPTER I

THE NATIONS AND UNIVERSAL HUMAN SOCIETY

I. *Man as a Social Being.*

" MAN is by nature a social being," the philosophers say, and the statement is accepted by the Church as expressing a truth of natural law. "Mankind is not a race of solitaries ; it is a man's very nature, apart from any act of decision, to live in society." [1]

It is physically necessary for man to live in society. Neither the child nor the adult can subsist without the aid of others, and thus without social relations. No man, left to his own individual efforts, could do more than subsist miserably, on a level inferior to that of the animals. In such a state of isolation there would be no possibility of developing the flourishing material civilization for which man's nature calls.

[1] Leo XIII, *Diuturnum Illud.*

Social life is, in the second place intellectually necessary for man's development. Science, art, learning, are essential parts of human life, but they are not the fruit of isolated work, they are essentially a collective possession, growing from generation to generation, and handed on from one individual to another.

Social life is, finally, necessary for the development of moral life. Man needs education to train and strengthen him, examples to guide him, counsels to advise him, and aid to succour him. And it is natural to him to worship and pray with his fellows.

Man cannot, therefore, attain to any full and harmonious development of his faculties without social aid. It is a natural and necessary means to human perfection and happiness, that is to say, to the realization of the human ideal.

We may go farther and say that the fulness and perfection of human life cannot be attained except through social relations. Physical life in its fulness demands to reproduce itself through procreation. The intellect of man is not satisfied with the mere possession of knowledge, it must propagate and spread what it knows. And our moral nature drives us to try to gain others to our own moral ideal, and strive to make it govern the world around us. The physical, intellectual and moral life of mankind seeks, in its perfection, to communicate itself to others.

Thus social relations are at once the necessary means towards human perfection and happiness, and the effect of our fulness of life.

Social life is, therefore, a primary and immediate demand of human nature. Life in society with others is natural, as it is the expression of the tendency of our nature; and is necessary, for without it our destiny, and our ideal life as human beings, cannot be realized. Man forms societies, that is permanent unions for a common purpose, in response to the impulses of his nature and the demands of his ideal of human life. The family on the one hand, the nation and the fatherland on the other, are the first of these natural societies.

2. *Nation and Fatherland.*

THE term " Fatherland " (like the Latin *Patria*, French *Patrie*) indicates a society which is distinguished by the idea of

continuity of successive generations,[1] and of
local continuity and stability through attachment to the land.

" Nation " is of similar meaning and origin :
nasci, to be born. " The Nation is the group
of those united by birth, descendants of the
same ancestors. It is almost the same thing
as the *patria* or Fatherland, but the latter
refers more especially to the country, the
nation more especially to the people." A
nomadic people has no " fatherland," but
can form a nation.

Patriotism, in its general sense, is the love
of one's country. It enriches and defines the
social instinct, by adding to it a natural
attachment to one's native land, to the race
whose blood flows in our veins, and to
the traditions linked with both of these.
Our country is the physical and human
milieu from which we spring and by
which we are nourished. It is, as St.
Thomas says,[2] at the basis of our existence
and our life : we are children of a people,
of a country, of a tradition, we owe to
them our existence and part of what we

[1] J. Leclerq, *Leçons de droit naturel*, vol 1. Brussels: Dewit,
1927, p. 230.
[2] St. Thomas, *Summa*, II^a, II^{ae}, Q. 101, art 1, art 3, ad 2um,
ad 3^m.

are, and like the love of father or mother or child, patriotism is an instinctive feeling that expresses our natural attachment to something with which our very being is bound up ; the sentiment or passion that it inspires is therefore perfectly legitimate.

But it is at the same time a moral virtue, by which man recognizes and pays his debt to the nation which has brought him to the light. Under this aspect, patriotism is simply an extension of filial piety. It is indeed by the practice of this virtue, says St. Thomas, that we render to those who engendered us the homage that we owe them. It is exercised on the one hand in the family, towards our parents and relatives, and on the other, in that " procreative " society, the Fatherland, towards our compatriots and towards nations that are friendly to or allied with our own.

Deriving from filial piety, the virtue of patriotism has a two-fold object : the service of the true interest of our country, and reverence and honour, by which we glorify it, thus expressing towards our country the homage that is part of piety. It inspires and stimulates the exercise of the virtue of general or social justice, which sees in the nation the common good of the citizens, the

3

natural basis and end of the State, and fixes our duties, as members of the community, towards the well-being of the society.

Our duty towards our country flows from the role and mission assigned to it by providence in human life. Catholic teaching seeks therefore to define the natural function of the nation, in order to appreciate its moral value and measure the duties of man in view of the claims it makes upon him.

3. *The Function of the Nation.*

Catholic thinkers see in the formation of nations a natural fact. By this we mean that nations correspond to the demands of the natural order of human life. This order is one willed by God, and conformable to the dispositions of His providence. The formation of nations, and the sentiments they inspire are therefore things good in themselves.

Like all that is providential in human life, the Nation should contribute to man's welfare. It fulfils a certain function in human life ; this function must be clearly defined in order to measure its value.

We may say, in general, that the Nation stabilizes and educates.

Man has need of the support and aid of

society. This mutual support is continuous through time, from generation to generation. There is a common mass of goods, economic (agricultural science and implements, etc.), physiological (race), intellectual, and moral, that grows and is transmitted from generation to generation. The individual thus finds, at his birth a heritage, a birthright at his disposal. The nation secures, throughout time, the continuity of the social goods necessary to the individual.

At the same time it furnishes him with an environment that keeps him from becoming a physical and moral nomad. It gives him a milieu to provide the physical, moral, and intellectual nourishment necessary for his life.

But how does the Nation act upon the individual ? How does it give him the goods that it has prepared and preserved for him ? By an influence that is partly creative, partly educative. It gives to the individual a body of manners and customs. That does not mean merely a certain number of habits or ways of doing things ; it implies a body of inclinations that become almost second nature. This is the value of the Nation. The national environment gives each one a nationality, that is to say a complex of physiological preformations and mental dispositions, from which result certain ways of seeing, thinking, and acting. Through nationality each one receives an ensemble of connatural manners which, in relation to the unqualified or merely potential original human nature, is an enrichment of it. Nationality puts the individual, without effort on his part, in possession of a certain measure of civilization, and raises him to a certain level of development. That is its natural and providential mission.

It is this mission that creates our moral obligation to the nation. From it man receives a heritage of civilization ; and in it he finds the social milieu necessary for his further development. He is bound to respect it as a means furnished by nature for the perfecting of himself and of others ; to injure or to destroy the nation would be to compromise his own destiny and that of his fellow-citizens. Everyone is bound, there-fore, to defend and foster his country, even at the peril of his life, " as long as it has not become evident that the continued exis-tence of that society has become harmful." [1]

[1] Leclercq, op.cit. p. 231.

From this it is clear that the nation never has an absolute, but always only a relative value. In itself, its value depends upon its usefulness to humanity; it is relative to the quality of the manners, mentality, disposition—the national formation—that it imparts to its members.

This concept of the providential function of the Nation, by which its value may be measured, enables us to judge of the deviations to which the idea of the Nation is exposed.

4. *False Conceptions of Nationalism.*

A. The first regards nationalism as having an ethnic or racial basis. It has many different forms, but all derive from one central conception.

It makes Nationality rest upon the blood-tie, upon the common tie of race. National unity derives principally from physiological characteristics transmitted by heredity. The rights of the nation are in reality those of a race: white or coloured, germanic, latin, slav, etc. In this theory humanity is explicitly or implicitly divided into peoples destined by nature to civilization and peoples inferior by nature; the first having, in comparison to the second, a position of greater rights and privileges.

This doctrine is ultimately a form of materialism ; and also, necessarily, one of conquest and racial domination : for the assertion of racial superiority and domination evokes a violent reaction on the part of others.

These racial theories err in basing the rights of a national group upon a mere physiological fact, the transmission of blood and the purity of the race, and in claiming that any such group has any rights over others. Race or blood gives no such rights. All men are equal in their essential character, as human beings endowed by Providence with the same rational and free nature, with one destiny and one transcendant ideal. Individual differences, due to race or blood, are irrelevant. The comparative nature and respective rights of nations are measured, not by qualities of blood or of race, but by the value of the civilization, and the culture which they transmit to the generations of their members, and by the manner and degree in which they contribute to the attainment of the human ideal.

B. Others base the rights of nations not

upon their natural mission, but upon the supposed autonomy and natural independence of the national will. It is the application to the nation, regarded as a unit of the principle of individualism. " The rights of man are based upon his autonomy, the faculty inherent in his nature to depend upon no will but his own in the direction of his thought and his acts." [1] The individual, in other words, has liberty and freedom; therefore he has rights. Applied to the nation this conception of rights gives each racial group an absolute right of political independence, in the name of the autonomy of the national being and will. The " principle of nationality," as it is thus most commonly conceived in these days, or the right of racial groups to political self-determination, is based implicitly on this conception of right. It is recognised by jurists and politicians that this " individualism " is likely to " destroy order and stability in the internal affairs of the State, and to create anarchy in international relations." [2]

National rights are based, neither upon the autonomy of racial groups or of their

---

[1] Beudant, le Droit individuel et l'Etat, p. 146.
[2] Report of the League of Nations Arbitrators in the case of Sweden v. Finland concerning the Aaland Islands.

collective wills, but upon the cultural mission which they have to fulfil towards their members. This gives the nation the right to demand security, help, and freedom to conserve, increase, and convey to its members the heritage of cultural values of which it is the guardian.

But political independence is not always and everywhere a *conditio sine qua non* for the fruitful fulfilling of this mission. The nation has not, therefore, an *absolute* right to independence, but a relative right, based upon the degree of liberty necessary for the achievement of its national aims ; often all it can claim is an ample meed of liberties, within the political framework of the State.

C. The conception of nationality is misunderstood by those—and they are many— who tend to regard any one form of nationality as absolute : the form that one knows most of and appreciates. National sentiment, one of the strongest of human passions, makes each one tend to regard as the ideal his own form of national culture. It is not remembered that each nation is the vehicle of a type of human culture, more or less elevated ; but that none fully expresses the ideal of human culture or civilization.

No given national culture may be identified with culture or civilization as such and absolutely ; for none is anything more than one possible form, a contingent consequence of historical development.

On the contrary we must hold that the realisation of man's ideal is not bound up, in any final and exclusive way, with any one particular form of nationality. Each national culture plays its part in the task, but none has the whole secret. That is why Catholicism, with the complete ideal of human nature before its eyes, is not essentially bound up with any national form, judging all by the value of their educative function, and seeing in all natural and providential supporters in the supernatural education which itself is destined to bring to mankind. It leaves to the people of countries most favoured by their respective nationality the duty of sympathizing with whatever measure or degree of the human ideal the other nationalities may embody. It points out to them the duty and obligation of endeavouring to enrich their own nationality (intellectually and spiritually), and of avoiding on the one hand immobilization in a national type

narrowly conceived, and on the other a
spirit of exclusiveness towards other national
types,

5. *Of International Relations. La Société Universelle.*

Nations are natural formations. But they
are constituted by particular, individual
influences—soil, climate, race, language,
religion, dynasty, history, etc., which differ-
entiate men, and give each group a special
type and stamp. But the essential human
nature is common to all ; it is not destroyed
by local peculiarities, but enriched and
adorned. Between the groups existing in
human nature, there must be relations : as
there is a society of men, so is there of nations.
So we have a larger community, which
transcends national boundaries, suprana-
tional, universal.

The society of nations has its foundation
in human nature itself. We may regard this
natural foundation in two ways. First, men
have the same human nature, therefore in
in their relations with one another they are
equal, peers one of the other. On the other
hand, their natural equality gives them
originally an equality of rights over the goods

of the earth. By the disposition of Providence the riches of the world were originally placed at the disposal of the whole human race, and every man may claim by natural right, subject to certain limitations, to use and benefit by them. Appropriation by individuals may legitimately determine this general right, and give rise to individual rights over certain things, But this does not affect the unity of all human nature, or the fact that all the goods of the earth are originally destined for all. And on this are founded international relations.

Human society as a universal grouping of all men is not inconsistent with the existence of particular national groups ; both are in accordance with human nature. There is no question of sacrificing one to the other, but they must be correlated in order of primacy. This is what is meant by international social relations.

If we consider the element in human nature that makes the nations, on the one hand, and universal human society on the other, we see that the latter derives from an essential trait of human nature : its identity in the whole race, and the duty of mutual aid and support which flows from it. The nation, on the other hand, owes its foundation to particular qualities of land, race, or history, contingent and variable, which add to, and are secondary to the essential in human nature. Hence the order of relation between the two societies : the national groups are subordinate to universal society.

Catholic thought, with its regard constantly fixed upon the universality of the Redemption, and on the natural equality of all men before their Saviour, was less likely than any other to lose sight of this unity which holds all men together in one society. It was a theologian of the sixteenth century, Vitoria, who at the moment when the nations and national states were being formed, saw clearly the existence of natural international society. He proclaimed that there existed " a natural right of society and communication," in virtue of which no racial group has the right to shut itself up jealously on its own soil and exclude all others from social participation in its natural resources. Under all natural differentiations there exists a natural right of human sociability, in virtue of which no local group can cut itself off from communication and exchange, commercial, industrial, intellectual, and moral. Natural law demands this widening of human life ; racial particularism has no prescriptive right against it.

We can now sum up the Catholic position in regard to nationalism and internationalism. To understand it, one must place oneself at the Catholic point of view, which is that of the human person and his perfectibility.

Catholicism is "nationalist," because the human individual needs for his proper development a milieu to nourish, guide, and teach him : this the nation gives him, and also marks him with its individual stamp.

But Catholicism is "internationalist." For the human being is also a person, the equal of any other by his rational and free nature and by his destiny, and so each has a right to enter into society with his fellows, and share with them in whatever there is of riches, of economic, spiritual, or moral value under whatever form of civilization it appears. In any form of nationalism devoid of the spirit of international sympathy, Catholicism sees an at least unconscious denial of the universality of the aspirations and possibilities common to all ; a denial of the spiritual nature of man, as a creature of intelligence and free will, that is tantamount to the

crudest materialism. It proclaims the
necessity and the moral duty to recognise
as well-founded both the institution of the
nation and of international organization ; and
also that the international institution which
unites the nations while respecting the
individuality of each, is ultimately the higher
of the two.

CHAPTER II

1. *States as Moral Persons and Subject to Law.*

As we have so far studied it, the Nation appears less as a society than as a social milieu in which individuals are born and from which they derive what is necessary for their lives. The national milieu acts on the individual through the culture and the character it imparts to him.

What marks the State, as distinct from the nation, is the presence of an authority, a power of Law, which unifies the group, binding together by rules of Law individuals and sections. The State acts upon the individual through the Law : it establishes a juridic order.

This authority has as its basis and as its aim the Common Good—or common weal, or public good, or public welfare ; which is the necessary condition for the private welfare of individuals and their private

31

groups. We may define it as " the totality of material and moral conditions which, in a natural and normal order permit persons so willing to endeavour to attain to temporal happiness, and the eternal happiness towards which this is ordained."

Because it is necessary for the physical and moral welfare of all, the common good has for each the force of moral obligation. It is for all, and each must serve it. Its demands create duties. These constitute an order of law—a legal or juridic order.

Further : being the good of all and sundry, it is superior to the good of the individual, and may legitimately subordinate this to itself.

The public authority is based on the common good, whose needs it expresses ; hence its power of law.

The National State—and most modern states are national—is not only a social milieu which imprints on those within it a nationality ; but also a society conscious of the need to govern for the Common Good, and of the will to realize it. It organises itself for its own benefit, gives itself organs of authority which, from being a nation, make it also a State. In virtue of this consciousness and this will, which have the common good as object, the State is a "moral personality," which, being aware of its aims and objects, organises itself with a view to attaining them.

The State is a " personality "—a definite, individual, living, unity ; a social body, composed of real factors, of individuals and groups united under a controlling authority in pursuit of their common and collective welfare ; and not a mere abstraction, or a handy label to denote a crowd, a number of persons who happen to be together, without interests or union.

It is a " personality " : that is to say it is conscious of its destiny and purpose, and is freely, with a sense of moral responsibility, seeking its object.

It is a "*moral* personality." The individual is a *physical* personality, because the bond that joins his members is physical, he is a physical unit. The State is a moral personality, because the bond that unites its members is a *moral bond :* knowledge of the common good, desire to submit to its demands by obedience to a rule of law.

We conclude then : the State is a moral personality, and is, therefore, a subject of Law.

4

The nation itself has rights as against those outside of it, because it is a natural formation fulfilling a providential mission for its members. It claims the respect of all others ; to hurt or destroy it would be to infringe the rights of its members. But only the State is, properly considered, a subject of Law. Only a person, physical and moral, deserves this title. It was not superfluous or a mere juridical technicality to show that the State is a moral personality, but a statement of its essential nature.

Relations between States must, therefore, be governed by the same rules as relations between other personalities.

2 *Moral Laws Governing Inter-State Relations.*

The laws governing the relations between States must be moral laws : for States are moral personalities. There is, therefore, a body of morals that governs international politics ; these are not to be left at the mercy or to the play of economic, military, or financial interests. States are made by men for their well-being, to help them to achieve their destiny. And so all political life, national or international, is subject to a moral standard, in harmony with the natural ideal of human life.

States are moral persons. And there are two virtues that govern the relations of persons : justice and charity, or good-will or friendship.

A. *Justice*—By justice we mean here the virtue that governs the relations of one legal subject to another : in these relations it ensures respect for the rights of the opposite party. It is based upon equality. In an exchange, it ensures equality of transference ; but it has also the much wider scope of respect for any kind of right of any other person.

Some rights of the State are based on its being an equal in law, and some on its being a moral person. As equal members of international society, States have the right to " their material personality, to their honour."[1] It is unjust, therefore, by the exercise of economic, military, or financial pressure to extract from a State concessions harmful to the vital interest of the community, without compensation or equivalent. And to defame or vilify a state, by words or acts, is also unjust.

[1] Valensin, *Semaines Sociales de France*, XVIIIth Session, 1926, La vie Internationale, p. 268.

Other rights of the State are based on its duty to ensure the common good of its nationals. These, as men, have the right to the peaceful possession of their share of the natural resources of the world, to commercial relations, exchange of raw material and manufactured goods, etc. States have political rights of the same order, based on their function as agents and representatives of their citizens. In the allotment of natural resources, and the organization of international trade and economics, the function of the State in regard to its nationals gives it a claim in justice for fair treatment.

Other obligations have as their basis an agreement made : *pacta servanda*. National self-interest can never make just the violation of a contract or infidelity to an agreement. No doubt, the international situation under which a given treaty was made may become different ; and then the details of the agreement may have to be revised. But it is one thing to revise an agreement in order to adapt it to a new situation, and another to violate it or denounce it, unilaterally. To enforce a treaty which needs revision, to stick to the letter of the law, may be the *summum jus* which might prove the *summa iniuria* ; but in the adaptation and revision itself, justice still governs the transaction.

It would, therefore, be a singular error to reduce all international justice to respect for treaties and contracts : it protects also rights that are prior to all contracts or conventions, the natural rights of the State, based on their own very nature and their natural function.

B. *Charity, or Mutual Aid and Support.* Justice has for its object the rights of the neighbour State, and ensures to it its due. Charity works for its well-being, and provides aid and support.

The word charity has in current usage a special derived sense. In Christian speech it has a precise and technical significance, which we must give it here. It denotes a virtue of the will, by which we desire the welfare of another as we desire our own. It is essentially a source of action, a motive force. It gives, in one word, but with deeper significance, what is expressed by such words as international solidarity, collaboration, co-operation,

Catholicism stresses the moral obligation of the States to mutual collaboration and co-operation, and shews as its basis its necessity for the proper accomplishment of their mission and function. '' It is the natural tendency of the human will to seek what the reason says is good. In social relations, this tendency shews itself through good-will, which makes us desire and seek for others what we desire for ourselves. That is the great principle that gives movement and life to the comity of nations. Without that *amor benevolentiae*, that disinterested charity and goodwill, there may be a union of peoples based upon self-interest ; but the approach will be like that of the gladiators of old, who drew closer to their opponents the better to destroy them by skill, by ruse, or by force. The society of nations is a union of minds and wills, and it must be governed by love and order. Take away from any society, love and good will, and there are left but the dry bones of its corpse." [1]

To the teaching of the natural law, as seen by the light of reason, Catholicism gives a new significance and a new basis. This collaboration and aid becomes, for the Catholic, part of the obligation of the supernatural law of Love on which rests the whole Christian moral order. All men of all peoples

[1] Taparelli, Essai théorique de Droit Naturel, II, I, VI, chap. 3.

were created for the same supernatural end ; and redeemed by the blood of the same divine Saviour : they are brothers in Christ. '' The Gospel,'' says Benedict XV.[1] '' has not one law of charity for individuals, and another for States and peoples.''

It is not as fantastic as it might sometimes seem, to consider international relations as really to be governed by charity. On the contrary, it is futile and utopian to imagine a real régime of international justice apart from the leavening and life-giving influence of charity. A spirit of mutual good will, understanding and sympathy is essential. Without it, even the clearest and most fundamental obligations in justice will be evaded, and the best guarantees useless. For justice is sterile and lifeless, unless charity give it life and vigour in the hearts of men. It is an interesting fact that in every country the wisest heads, the most detached and least sentimental observers, are to-day appealing for a spirit of European or even world co-operation, with a view to such collaboration as is not demanded by bare justice. States feel more than ever the need of what we call by its Christian name, Charity. It is a

[1] Pacem, 23rd May, 1920.

further fact that this virtue of collaboration has shown itself efficaciously in international politics during recent years, sometimes in an unmistakable fashion, sometimes in a less noisy but more useful way. One might mention, for instance, the financial reconstruction of Austria and of Hungary, the loans to Greece and to Bulgaria in favour of the refugees, etc.

Catholicism refuses to separate justice from charity, international legal obligations from the obligations of international co-operation and interdependence ; and re-affirms the twofold ideal of justice and friendship all the more firmly, because it knows how to make them effective.

In the last analysis, the obligations of justice and charity that bind the State, become incumbent upon the individuals who make up a State. States can act only through their individual citizens and rulers : there is no impersonal agent, but only individual men, and every one of those has a conscience. " It is consciences that must be given discipline," said Pius XI., in his Encyclical *Ubi Arcano Dei*. Hearts must be opened to a mutual sense of fraternal charity and justice. Catholic morality holds no man just, though he may be never so exact in his personal and national obligations, if he fails in his international duties ; nor charitable, if he be kind and charitable to his own but cherish hatred against another people. If international relations are to be governed by moral considerations, these must be planted in the souls of the individual citizens, with a sense of their personal responsibility. Merely to proclaim ideals of international understanding, of amity and co-operation between nations, is futile unless the conscience of the world can be stirred to implement them. Catholicism, and it only, can do both. It is in a position to formulate a moral code, because it has at its disposal the means of influencing the conscience of citizens and their rulers alike. That is its duty, its mission.

CHAPTER III

INTERNATIONAL SOCIETY

So far we have considered the mutual relations of States as being acts of juridical personalities, governed by principles of justice and charity. These are personal and, so to speak, private relations, the relations of individuals between themselves, each State retaining its full independence and sovereign status, and being bound only to respect the rights of others and to furnish to its equals the benevolent aid that every being owes to its kind.

In addition to these private relations of justice and benevolence, states may be incorporated into a larger political framework, in which each becomes a part, member or unit of an international body possessing in itself a principle of order and of authority.

In this case, a new situation is created for the member-states, with new rights and duties. There is a real international society, a social body, and not merely persons or individuals privately related. What characterizes a society as a distinct body is the union of the members for a common end which is the centre of thought and effort ; it is the existence of a common good to which all members are bound to contribute. The necessary means towards this common end become the law of the society, the rule of action of the members, who are now members of a body to which they owe obedience : social obligation has taken the place of independence and isolation. The rules of interindividual morality remain, but now there are added *the duties of social and of distributive justice.*[1]

1. *The Basis of International Society.*

Formerly it was the tendency of jurists and of the law to lay stress especially upon the independence of states. Inspired by the teaching of Aristotle, legal doctrine saw in the state—the City—a self-sufficing community. St. Thomas defines it : a society

---

[1] Distributive justice and social justice exist only within a Society, the former distributes equitably social rights and advantages between the members, in proportion due to each according to his rank or station. It distributes the common good. The second regulates the duties of the individual towards the community in so far as he is a member of it. It determines our obligations in respect of the common good.

which procures for its members the complete
good of human life. Such a society should
normally suffice for all human needs : and
seems, therefore, to be essentially independent. This conception corresponded adequately
enough to the facts of the case, as long as
the state of civilization lasted in which most
countries could live almost entirely each on its
own resources, only luxuries and articles of
secondary importance being imported from
abroad. And so, in determining the rights
and duties of states, jurists and moralists
reasoned from the data : the state is a self-
sufficing community. But we must be
careful before deducing from this the right
of absolute independence or isolation.

In this conception, there is room only for
inter-individual moral relations between
states.[1] But the absolute independence of
political societies, never perfectly realized,
is to-day more than ever a dream. The very
first of the Catholic thinkers who saw before
them the modern national state, recognized
that it could not be self-sufficing. " If every
state, republic or kingdom, constitutes a

[1] Christendom was, it is true, a higher universal society of
which the states were members, but it was not a natural
political formation based upon the nature of the state : it was
founded on their common Christian faith.

perfect community," says Suarez, " it is not the less sure that these communities could not suffice unto themselves if completely isolated. They must, therefore, for their good and development, enter into certain relations of aid and fellowship with each other."[1]

To-day economic relations have become multiplied to an indefinite extent. " Nothing and no one can keep out of the current. The most remote Breton peasant drinks coffee from Brazil, reaps his harvest with a machine from Chicago, sells his butter and apples in London. The humblest cell vibrates in accord with the universal rhythm." [2]

It is the same with the exchange and communication of thought and feeling. Sitting quietly in our study, we can hear without effort a sermon from Notre-Dame in Paris, a concert from New York, or a presidential pronouncement from Pekin. The more civilization develops, the closer and the more necessary become the solidarity and interdependence of each state with the rest of the world. This strengthening of

[1] Suarez. *De legibus*, Book ii, ch. 19, No, 9.
[2] Francis Delaisi : *Les contradictions du monde moderne*, Paris, 1925, p. 543.

interdependence is, as we see, simply due to the nature of man and of the case.

But as culture and civilization develops, each racial group becomes more and more conscious of its own distinctive qualities, and these become more and more dear to it as that appreciation is refined. It attaches itself more closely to its soil, its traditions, its customs, its language. National temperaments become more tense, and patriotism more ardent. Under the influence of this awakening consciousness, and this more lively attachment, the groups tend to form themselves into states, so that the multiplicity of states itself appears as a fruit of the development of humanity. If states become less, and less self-sufficing, that is very far from meaning that they are in the way of disappearing or being absorbed by others.

An evolution of a different kind, but balancing this double process of development, is the formation of the League of Nations, a group of moral personalities—states or dominions—possessed of autonomy, but now brought together by their vital needs and the exigencies of their existence. This League is not set up at the expense of the constituent states, destroying their entity, but for their gain, to the benefit of their mission and function, and the increase of their vitality. Respectful of all legitimate national differences, it seeks to create a human order everywhere organized and correlated, by the juridic grouping of states, who are moral persons possessed of political freedom.

This League of Nations which is in process of development before our eyes is then a political superstructure, established over the states or particular societies. It is a society naturally derived, in the sense that it finds its basis in the very nature of the national states and serves their needs. It is, therefore, not created simply by a mutual pact or contract : it has its basis in natural law, which gives it a principle of order.

2. *The Principle of Order in International Society.*

Interstate relations are not a mere fact, developing under the drive of historical necessity or the pressure of interest. They are ultimately related to the ideal of itself that each state pursues, and are, therefore, subject to the moral order, out of which can arise a positive juridic order.

A. The state has a natural mission to fulfill towards its citizens : to provide them with the ensemble of social conditions necessary to a free and happy life, all that is necessary for their full mental, moral, and material development. This is impossible without international exchanges and relations: these, therefore, are necessary to the state for the fulfilling of its purpose. We may say of the State what is rightly said of man : as man cannot isolate himself from society without renouncing his natural destiny, so also the state cannot renounce international relations without renouncing the mission it has towards its citizens. On the idea of a natural purpose of the state is founded the idea of an obligation with the imperative force of an idea, binding and chaining it to life in Society.

But in its turn this interstate life needs organs of its own. In every domain of international activity, whether it be political or economic, scientific or philanthropic or moral, it must have machinery of some kind, organs to regularise, co-ordinate, and assure cooperation. Through these, interstate society takes concrete existence ; it can act and secure the rights of the common international good.

The common good of the State is an ensemble of rules, institutions, relations and organisations, that facilitates and ensures a co-operation through which justice and peace in interstate relations are guaranteed.

All states benefit thereby : all of them, by their very nature, have need of it. All must have recourse to it ; all are bound to contribute to and serve it. The common good constitutes, in the interstate society, a principle of order and of obligation.

The obligations of the states to international Society are first moral obligations, binding the consciences of peoples and of governments. They must conform to the exigencies of the common international good, first because it is the condition necessary for the accomplishment of their own natural ideal, and, secondly, because being the good of all, it takes priority over the good of the individual, and may subordinate it to itself. The states must, therefore, not only abstain from anything that might compromise the common good, but must work positively to promote it, in the measure that the state of civilization and of historical evolution, by increasing the degree of interdependence, have made mutual aid necessary. If it is sometimes difficult as yet to make people realize this moral obligation, it is because they do not see how impossible it is for the state to function properly in a state of isolation,—and also because this impossibility, the fruit of the development of civilization, is a relatively new thing and is still in evolution.

The obligations of the states towards their common good is not a mere echo of their moral duties towards humanity in general : they make these concrete, with reference to a given situation. As, for example, for a French, Italian, or Chinese citizen the virtue of patriotism gives precision and definition to the social instinct with which they were born, and gives them definite duties towards a definite society, so we may say that the duties of states towards the interstate society are, in any given historical situation, a more clearly defined aspect of the general obligations of men to their fellows, and, more immediately, of the states towards humanity and civilization.

B. These moral obligations can, finally, furnish the basis of juridic obligations of positive law : they enable a juridic order to be constituted within international society.

According as, owing to the effect of the

increasing interdependence of peoples, interstate society comes into being, a juridic order must arise within it to state in concrete rules with positive sanction the international moral order. Hence a twofold duty for states.

1°. They must take part in the juridic organisation of the interstate life, to the degree in which the facts and the situation make this possible and necessary. States are *free* agents : not that they may do as they please, but that they act with knowledge and a power of choice, in other words with a sense of responsibility. They are free, in the sense that they must make a wise choice of the best ways and methods ; their freedom is ruled by duty, and exists for the better doing of the task.

2°. When the exigencies of the common good are expressed in positive rules, these become law that binds the States, as the law binds the conscience of the individual citizen in any particular state.

Thus should be constituted a League of Nations, in which a legal order reigns, based upon the moral order. The formation of an organized society, in which the component states retain their political liberty as free moral personalities, under an authority given such power as the common good ordains, seems the natural solution of the problem caused by the factual interdependence and political individualism of the states. What juridic form this society would take it is impossible to foresee. Its evolution will depend upon many factors, some arising out of economic and political development, and some out of free decisions by human wills. No man can say how it will come. But it is already a great deal to know that such a society has its roots in the very nature of humanity, and that it has its natural law, the principles of its organisation, its authority and its ideal.

CHAPTER IV

PEACE

1. *Peace.*⧣⧣Hobbes defined peace as " the absence of war." That is an incomplete, nay a false idea of peace.

Peace is tranquillity in order.[1] In the complex unity of an organism, each part must occupy the place, and do the work assigned to it by nature for the common good. The whole forms an ensemble in which order reigns : the action of each part is subordinated to the common good and co-ordinated with that of the other parts. There results a state of harmony and of happy activity which is characteristic of the reign of order. Peace is a name for that state of harmonious collaboration of parts, diverse in nature and importance, for a common aim, and the happiness which it brings for the whole and for each of the members.

[1] Pax omnium rerum, tranquillitas ordinis, St. Augustine, de civ. Dei, XIX. c. 13.

Peace is an effect, therefore : the result of respect for order.

2. *International Peace.*—In International society, peace comes from the respect of international order.   In what does this order consist ?

(*a*) First in respect for the rights of every state, in the name of justice.   Every violation of the rights of a people is contrary to order, and destroys peace, even if it do not take the form of effective measures of armed hostility.   For international peace is not simply a material tranquility in the relations of states : it is, and more profoundly, the realization of an order of law, spiritual and moral, of which material tranquility is only the outward expression.

(*b*) But if the respect for the rights of others is necessary for peace, it is not itself peace : it does not alone make peace, but is rather a negative condition of peace. "Peace," says St. Thomas, "is indirectly the product of justice, in the sense that justice removes all obstacles to it." [1]

Peace demands a positive collaboration of states in view of their common good.   It could not be otherwise : the natural inter-

[1] IIᵃ, IIᵃᵉ, q. XXIX, Art 3, ad. 3.

national order is not a state of isolation in which each state remains barricaded within its frontiers, enjoying an absolute and wild independence. If that were so, peace would simply be a matter of avoiding trespass. But the reality is otherwise : each state needs the help of others, and is itself bound to them. The natural interstate order is one of collaboration. For peace then is required a positive accord of wills, a common activity, co-ordinated and planned in view of the common good of all.

According as people become more closely related, international order becomes more clearly an order of interdependence, and peace becomes more and more a matter of willing collaboration. It demands that in addition to the particular justice that governs the relation of individual states, there should be created a higher form of social interstate justice, to regulate the contribution of each state to the common good ; and a distributive justice to ensure to each state its due share in the common advantages, and its due place in the ensemble of the international body. No one can believe, in view of the present state of the world, that individual arrangements between states can ensure peace. Peace, in our day, is less than ever a matter of mere reciprocal neutrality : it is essentially a matter of mutual aid and collaboration.

3. International peace is not simply the product of positive international law, or of politics, the art of government. International positive law has a limited field, viz., international justice. Politics has a wider scope, for it is governed by the two virtues that rule the relations of states, justice and charity.

But international juridic and political peace rests on deeper foundations. International order is the consequence of peace established in each state, and firmly grounded within each nation, between the classes and the groups that form them, and finally in the souls of the individual citizens, by the reign of moral law. International peace must have firm foundations, must be the culmination of the reign of peace in every degree of human life. And so it can only be perfectly and ideally realized if it is identical with the reign of supernatural justice and peace, in harmony with the supernatural vocation of humanity. In this sense, Christ is truly the God of peace, and the Church the home and source of peace.

4. As peace is synonomous with international order, it represents the normal mutual relationship of states, that is to say, the order that corresponds to their fundamental function and purpose. As such it is the ideal towards which the efforts both of nation and persons should strive : to maintain the peace that exists, to repair it if it has been violated. The realization of ideals is, however, contingent and problematic. The ideal of peace is especially so. It is sometimes the case that in a given place social justice and positive collaboration are not sufficiently assured.—that is a surface disturbance, so to speak. But sometimes also social, economic or moral disorder causes a deep-seated cancer in a state or in several states, and creates a permanent and dangerous menace to the whole fabric of international peace.

CHAPTER V

WAR

It would be quite erroneous to regard peace and war from the same point of view, as two sides of an alternative. Peace is order, and, therefore, the normal state of things, that which would always be if men did not fail in the observance of justice and charity. War, as opposed to peace, finds no place in international order, except alone when it is a work of justice. But when is this the case ? To answer that question is the object of the present chapter.

1. *The Nature of War.*

States, being moral personalities, have rights and duties. From this point of view, we can regard them as individuals. If injured in their essential rights, they have, therefore, the right, and the duty, to defend themselves. Thus considered war seems to be the application of the saying : Vim vi repellere omnia iura permittunt.[1]

---

[1] It is always lawful to repel force by force.

58

But this individualistic conception of war does not take into account its true nature. In defending itself and its citizens, the state re-establishes order, the universal order upon which its own particular rights are based. Now in thus re-establishing universal order, in vindicating the Right, it fulfills a mission proper to it and inherent in its nature. For it is, here below, the guardian of justice. It is the supreme power, exercising vindicative justice : that is, the form of justice on which penal law is founded ; this consists in punishing the criminal in the name of a higher order of morality.

There is an order of law that applies to international life ; theologians are unanimous in seeing in the belligerent state a minister of international order. It performs an act of jurisdiction that has as its purpose the punishment of the criminal and the re-establishment of the Right : it fulfills a function that belongs only to a supreme authority : that is to say, to God in respect of the whole world, to public authority in regard to human societies.[1]

From this conception of war we can see

[1] It follows that soldiers who kill in battle are not murderers ; they execute a just sentence.

what conditions must be present to make it just and lawful.

2. The Conditions of a Just War.

It must be declared by the legitimate authority. It is an executive procedure, carried out in the name of the law, within a properly constituted society. It follows that it must be decided and accomplished by the legitimate authority.

But what this legitimate authority is, depends upon the mode of organisation and the actual state of international society at the given moment.

Because war is an act of supreme jurisdiction, the right to declare it belongs to the sovereign responsible for public order. Before the constitution of the modern states, in the feudal epoch, for instance, when there was no effective central authority, it was a problem to know when any particular baron, prince, or city authority had sufficiently the responsibility for order to justify them in claiming the right of war and the exercise of supreme vindicative justice. The constitution of modern states, under the authority of definite sovereigns, makes the question superfluous nowadays. The responsibility

for order and the right of war belongs
obviously to the head of the sovereign state
and to him only, for he has in his hands the
supreme powers of the state, and, consequently, the mission to maintain order.
This is, generally speaking, the situation in
the modern world.

We must, however, point out that this
situation tends to be modified, and that we
can already see the lines of a slow but real
evolution. International relations become
more and more complex, states become more
and more interrelated and interdependent ;
and the whole idea of sovereignty must be
modified to meet the new situation. As long
as there was no higher jurisdiction to protect
law and right, responsibility for public international order rested upon the individual
states and gave them the right and duty to
defend it. But in the measure that politico-
social evolution makes the states into members
of a larger body, created by their common
vital needs, the responsibility for assuring
order among the members of this international society tends to pass to this latter.
And reciprocally, in the measure that international institutions or international practice
shews that something of this kind has

happened and offers new possibilities of mediation, conciliation or arbitration, a moral duty is imposed on states, obliging them to have recourse to these methods, whenever they are able to provide, as a means for the enforcement of right, an alternative to war.

Similarly, arbitration or conciliation treaties between states make it unlawful and unjust for these to declare war without having had recourse to the means of solving their differences prescribed in their agreements. Members of all societies are bound to avail themselves of the procedure fixed by the lawful authority, instead of taking the law into their own hands, when they have suffered unjust loss or damage ; international treaties and compacts seek to establish as between states, a new procedure as an alternative to war. This once established becomes the only lawful or just one.

B. *The just cause.* War may not be declared by the lawful authority unless there be just cause for it. Those whom one attacks must, says St. Thomas, have deserved it by some fault. It could not be otherwise, because war is the assertion of justice against a criminal. As Vitoria says : the one and only just cause of war is the violation of right.

(1) Ambition ; the desire for political or economic conquests ; the endeavour to re-inforce authority by diverting attention to external affairs ; the propagation of religion or civilization : such reasons do not justify war, though they have often caused or have been made to excuse it.

(2) No war can be just on both sides. No doubt, in international affairs there is often so much confusion of reciprocal rights and duties, that in the absence of any disinterested tribunal to judge of the rights of the conflicting parties, each side is in good faith in thinking that it is in the right. But right must be on one side or the other.

(3) At the beginning of every war, there-fore, there is a question of right to be decided. In the interest of their common peace and justice, there should be established by the states a system of juridic and political tribunals to pronounce upon such questions, and so settle without armed conflict the issues that arise. There are many possible ways of doing this : an international Court of Justice, arbitration courts, etc.

In default of such institutions, the question of right appertains for decision to the state

heritage of human culture will be seriously compromised or impaired, then war is not ordained towards peace, but towards destruction of peace. The good or right of a particular state is not the highest good : there are cases in which the state must put the general good before its own strict right, and subordinate its own individual claims to higher values, to interests of a higher moral or spiritual order.

Granted the rightness of intention,—and Catholic doctrine makes it a fundamental presupposition for a just war—it is not difficult to state how a just war may be conducted without prejudice to humane interests.

Since the re-establishment of peace and order is the sole motive of the belligerents, they must avoid all measures that would bring upon the innocent the sufferings of war.

Further, they must adapt their conduct to the purpose of their actions ; not even upon those responsible for the war may they inflict suffering that is not a means towards peace and right. Justice must be enforced, of course, and the greater the resistance to it, the more force, the more violence must be used to overcome that unjust resistance. But even war, among civilized peoples, can be made less barbarous than it might be. Certain weapons can be excluded ; arrangements can be made to secure the interests of non-combatants, of the sick and wounded etc. And any international obligations entered into in this connection are binding on the conscience of the belligerents.

Out of this conception of war two conclusions emerge : since war is an effort towards peace and order, it should be as least cruel as possible ; and also, for the same reason, the nations should show their progressive sense in putting forward the ideal of an alternative to war—something that were less unworthy of mankind, less fraught with inhuman and unnecessary horrors. Those who believe in a national progress of nations and peoples may work for an alleviation of the terrors of war and for its gradual elimination. But the reversion of even one nation to the barbaric mentality of war will make necessary on the part of its opponents all that is implied in war. The one and only thing that will stop, or, at least, regulate war is the development of the moral sense and the spirit of religion.

3. *Treaties of Peace.*

" Since the object of war is peace, war must cease as soon as a durable and definite peace is obtainable. A just war may not be transformed into a war of conquest under the pretext of preventing a recrudescence of attack,—but with the real purpose of completely subjugating a people which has a right to independence.

The purpose of the peace treaty is the restoration of law and order. It can and should, according to the moralists, be based on the following principles ; but the concrete application of these is susceptible of many modifications.

(a) It must bring reparation of the right the violation of which started the conflict ; (b) compensate for the losses which the just belligerent suffered in the conflict ; (c) inflict just punishment on the guilty party ; (d) assure, by adequate guarantees, durable peace and order.[1]

The peace which puts an end to war should be a return to international order, that is to say, to justice and co-operation. The treaty must, in other words, be a

---

[1] Tanqueray, *op. cit.*, p. 238.

charter of justice, and render possible the
resumption of the normal relations of mutual
aid and support. As Vitoria said in the 16th
century : When war is declared for a just
cause, it must be conducted not to destroy
the nation against which it is waged, but to
obtain what is due ; to defend the fatherland
and the state, and secure peace and justice.
It were the essence of cruelty to seek, and to
be glad to find, reasons to justify killing and
destroying men whom God created and for
whom Christ died. War must be waged
only under direct compulsion. When victory
has terminated the war, the victory must be
used with Christian moderation and modesty :
the victor must act as a judge pronouncing
between two states, one of which has violated
the right of the other ; and it is as a judge,
not as a accuser, that he must pronounce
the sentence that re-establishes justice in
favour of the injured party. Further :
penalties must be restricted, and be as lenient
as possible ; while the guilty must be
punished, the guilty state must be treated
as mildly and as indulgently as possible." [1]

[1] Vitoria, *de jure belli.*

PART II

THE WORK OF THE CATHOLIC CHURCH FOR PEACE [1]

[1] In compiling these pages we have drawn our inspiration directly from the following works :—

Battifol, Monceaux, Chenon, Vanderpol, Rolland, Duval, Tanquerey, *L'Eglise et la Guerre*. Paris, Bloud, 1913.

G. Goyan, *L'Eglise Catholique et le droit des Gens*. Académie de droit international. Extrait du Recueil des Cours. (Paris Hachette) 1926.

Frederic Duval, *De la paix de Dieu à la paix de fer* (Paris, Paillard), 1923.

Yves de la Brière, S.J., *L'Organisation internationale du monde Contemporain et la Papauté Souveraine*. (Paris, Editions Spes.) 1924 and 1928.

PART II

THE WORK OF THE CATHOLIC CHURCH FOR FRANCE

CHAPTER I

EARLY CHRISTIAN TIMES

THE idea of Peace founded upon Justice, which is one of the essential ideas of the evangelical message, was not destined to remain at the theoretical stage in the Catholic Church. From the earliest days of Christianity it manifests itself as one of the preoccupations of the Heads of the Church, and of the faithful of Jesus Christ. It has not ceased since then to work as a driving force through the course of the whole life of the Church. It has dictated all her measures and determined her attitudes.

The earliest Christians prayed for peace. At the end of the first century Pope Saint Clement of Rome asked God " to give to us and to all the inhabitants of the earth, Peace and Concord . . . , to direct the Counsel of Princes in accordance with what is right and pleasing to Him so that exercising peaceably, piously, and with toleration the Authority which God has given them, He may graciously hear their prayers." Certainly, there could have been no question of the disciples of Christ making war upon war. It would have been an attempt to upset the whole political and social organisation, and to reduce the Roman Empire to anarchy. The teachings of Christianity did not insist upon the suppression of war, any more than, in the beginning, on the abolition of Slavery ; it only laid down the principles which were later to lessen fratricidal strife and its excesses.

It would seem at first sight that military careers should have been forbidden to Christians.   There were intolerant minds, urged by an uncomprising logic who expounded this, such as Tertullian in the second century, Origen in the third century, Lactantius in the fourth century. These had no followers. If, during a certain period, access to the higher grades was forbidden to Christians by ecclesiastical authority, this was because of the necessity which might have arisen for them to take part in the ceremonies of the worship of idols, or, to pronounce sentences of death.   With this exception, tradition, on the whole, accepted war as a fact, military service as a public service which had nothing essentially incompatible with the service of Jesus Christ.

This became, moreover, a necessity when the Empire found itself attacked on all sides by the barbarians. These hordes of invaders who threatened to submerge the whole of civilisation had to be opposed by an armed resistance. Nevertheless war was not indiscriminately permitted nor without provision against excesses. It had to be just. And it was just, when its object was to defend the country against barbarians ; it had to be kept within the bounds of prudence, moderation, magnanimity. Peace itself which was its goal had to be ordered by justice. Such was the doctrine that Saint Ambrose expounded at the end of the fourth century, and it was followed, at the beginning of the fifth century, by St. Augustine's definition of the essential points of the teaching of the Church in these matters.

CHAPTER II

THE BARBARIAN INVASIONS AND THE
MEROVINGIAN PERIOD

In the early middle ages, during the long
period opening with the fall of the Western
Roman Empire, and closing with its restoration by Charlemagne, war prevailed everywhere. Foreign tribes from every direction
crossed the Roman frontiers. Some of them
were still pagans, and this fact explains their
opposition to Christian activities for peace.
Of those who were converted a certain number
became heretics ; far from allowing themselves to become imbued by the charity of
Christ, they found in their efforts new
stimulus for hatred. Of the barbarians who
embraced Catholicism and who were baptised
many were not yet penetrated by the spirit
of Christianity. It was all the more difficult
to imbue them with that spirit because of
the civil quarrels raging all around them,
and of never ending wars in which all the
horrors of the old order of things constantly

recurred. The priests and the bishops taught them that human life was sacred ; the Councils exhorted them to forget injuries, to become reconciled with their enemies. They even went as far as threatening with excommunication those who refused to obey so holy an injunction. These interpreters of the Catholic Doctrine were scarcely listened to : passions were too strong. Edifying, on the other hand, was the admirable example given by those communities of men who lived during the Empire, under a religious rule, and who practised among other virtues the virtue of charity. Peace, which Saint Benedict, the patriarch of monastic life, gave as a law and motto to his disciples, reigned in the monasteries before it spread over the world : its lessons were most eloquent in countries laid waste by discord.

In the midst of a society torn by wars, the heads of the Catholic Church were animated by a strong spirit of that peace and love which ought to reign among the members of the great human family. It was the Bishop of Seville, Saint Leander, who exclaimed in 598, in the Second Council of Toledo :—" Holy Church of God, rejoice.

Knowing how sweet is your charity, how beautiful is union, you preach only harmony among nations, you sigh only for the union of races.   Nature intends that all peoples being descendants of a common ancestor, should be bound together by mutual love." [1]

The head of the Roman Church, Saint Gregory the Great, put into practice the words of the Spanish Bishop, when, some years later, at the end of the sixth century, he encouraged the efforts of those who worked to restore peace between the States, when he invited the new nations to become members of the Christian Republic, a Christian republic, which, as envisaged by him, an old Roman, could only be the former Roman Empire still existing in Constantinople.

[1] Migne, *Patrologie latine*, tome LXXII., Col. 895.

CHAPTER III

THE FEUDAL PERIOD

WHEN, in the beginning of the ninth century, unity had been restored in the whole Western World by the powerful hand of Charlemagne, when the restoration of the Empire by the Head of the Roman Church had in some measure ensured that it would last, it seemed as if Peace were about to reign in all these regions. The powerful emperor only tolerated wars which aimed at the spread of civilisation. He devoted himself to the maintenance of order and justice, and to the protection of the weak, within the empire. His new title imposed upon him the duty of being, after God and the Saints, the protector of Churches, of orphans, pilgrims, and widows. But with the end of his reign, peace also ceased to reign. A new period of widespread anarchy began, a period in which was to be witnessed the Great Emperor's Son, Louis (le Débonnaire), quarrelling with his own children. It was then that the Roman pontiffs intervened as supreme guardians of peace. To those who denied him this right of intervention, Gregory IV. replied : " How can you oppose me as well as your churches when I am fulfilling a mission of peace and unity which is a gift of Christ and Christ's Ministry itself. Do you not know that the Angels sang that Peace was promised to men of good will. Christ must dwell in the heart of all the faithful, and His spirit must preserve their unity by the bond of peace," His successor, Sergius III., threatened with Canonical punishment those princes " who prefer to follow the prince of discord, and are not willing to remain within the peace of the Catholic Church." Nicholas I., the great Pope of the ninth century, only carried on the tradition of his predecessors when he claimed the right to approach the Secular Powers to preach Concord and Peace to them. He only considered war permissible when it was just : " It is always satanic in its origin, he declared to the Bulgarians, and it must always be refrained from. But, if it cannot be avoided ; if it is a question of defending ourselves or our country or the laws of our fathers, there is no doubt that we may prepare for it even in Lent."

Nevertheless the power of the monarchy continued to become weaker under the Carlovingians. The lords freed themselves from the king. They took up arms to fight the new invaders : in the East, it was the Hungarians who crossed the Rhine and overran France ; in the West, the Normans arrived by sea and sailed up the rivers, spreading terror and desolation everywhere. The danger over, these lords armed against the pirates remained at war with the people. They had not lost the habit of raids, fights, adventures, and soon they were joined by all the outcasts of social life : fugitives, emigrants, the unfortunate of all kinds who had no other means of livelihood than plunder. Usurpations, depredation, murder, all these evils from which Gaul had suffered in the fifth century, and in the sixth, descended once more upon her. The world returned to the reign of force. Everything was at the mercy of the powerful and cunning. An energetic and resolute adventurer held a piece of territory or an " honour " at the point of the sword. " Such terrible evils have spread over the kingdom " said the Bishops assembled at Piste, in 862, to the King, " that we can

7

cry out with the prophet : ' Strangers ravage our lands, under our very eyes ; the sword has penetrated to the soul.' " Mournful lamentations re-echoed constantly in the Councils, in the writings, in the laws.[1] We may add that owing to the lack of sufficient central power, the lords were a law unto themselves. A regime of private wars was established, a system of reprisals and revenge which wasted the country. " Wars, armies, enemy raids, increase in number to such a degree," wrote Saint Peter Damien in the middle of the eleventh century, " that a greater number of men perish by the sword than by disease and infirmity."

1. *The Protection of the Weak and the Peace of God.*

The Church intervened in the chaos of feudal anarchy to re-establish the respect of law and to impose Peace. Already, on many occasions, in the course of the tenth century, particularly in the province of Reims, the bishops had concerned themselves in their assemblies with the protection

---

[1] G. Hanotaux, *Histoire de la Nation française,* tome III. *Histoire Politique des Origines à 1515,* par P. Imbart de la Tour, p. 248.

of monasteries and churches against the attacks of the lords. At the end of the tenth century they threatened with excommunication those who ignored the interdicts. The Council of Narbonne in 900 had decreed it against those guilty of invading church property, or using violence against members of the clergy. The Council of Anse (near Lyons) had pronounced it against those who attacked the abbey of Cluny and its inhabitants. This was found insufficient. It became necessary to extend the benefits of ecclesiastical protection to the ordinary faithful, to all those who were not engaged in war. This was done in the Assembly held in 989 in the monastery of Charroux in the diocese of Poitiers. In the presence of their clergy and of their faithful, having implored the help of Divine intervention, the bishops of the province of Bordeaux not only prohibited, again, armed raids upon churches and attacks on the clergy : they pronounced anathema against those guilty of robbing the peasant or poor of his sheep, oxen, or asses. The following year, in 990, in a Council which assembled at Puy, and at which there were present bishops from the provinces of Embrun, Vienne and Narbonne, the Protection of the Church

was extended to the merchant ; they promulgated at it, in the form of statutes
(*charta de treuga et pace*) measures similar
to those that the Bishop of Puy had got
his flock to take, fifteen years before.

In these troubled times when force pre-
dominated, the respect of the right, the
maintenance of peace could only be assured
by force. The church did not hesitate to
have recourse to it. In 997, at the Council
of Limoges ; in the year 1000 especially, at the
Council of Poitiers, the first associations for
Peace were organised under its auspices.
It was decided that in future any dispute
would be settled according to right. Against
anyone wishing to use violence, the bishops
or the Court could demand the co-operation
of all those who, having been present at the
Council, had entered into the Pact of Peace.
The King of France, Robert the Pious,
gave his assent to these beginnings : he
encouraged them. He himself presided in
Orleans at Christmas 1010, at an assembly
of lords and bishops who, in their turn,
proclaimed Peace. In 1016 the lords of
Burgundy, the Archbishops and bishops of
the provinces of Lyons and Besançon met
in Assembly, or in Council, at Verdun-Sur-

Doubs, were not satisfied with merely pledging themselves to maintain peace ; they took solemn oaths on the relics of the saints to respect churches and persons consecrated to God ; to refrain from taking cattle, from imprisoning peasants and merchants ; from setting fire to houses ; from uprooting vines ; from destroying mills ; from attacking the peasant when carrying away the product of his vines. Those guilty of violating this peace, or failing to take the necessary oaths to keep it before the feast of Saint Peter (29th June) were threatened with excommunication. What was done at Verdun-Sur-Doubs was repeated at other Councils. The holy relics were brought to them, to win the adherence of the refractory. It was said " If the fomenters of evil will not make peace through respect for and fear of the king, let them at least sign the Pact of Concord in the name of God and of His saints whose relics are here present." [1] Against the rebellious punishments as severe as the interdict were pronounced. The Council of Limoges in 1031 decided that if the nobles remained rebellious to Peace proposals, the whole country would be excommunicated,

[1] Paster, *Etudes sur le règne de Robert le Pieux.*

with the exception of the clergy, strangers, and children of under two years of age, all would be denied Christian burial. The Altars would be stripped of their ornaments, the Services would be celebrated in mourning. The Sacraments would not be administered except to the dying. For a people who had faith no punishment could have been more terrible. Every day prayers were offered for Peace.

The system for the defence and protection of peace was made still more complete in 1038, when, at the Council of Bourges, "a sort of National Guard, whose duty was to hold in check the feudal lords," was inaugurated.[1] The Archbishop of Bourges, Aimon, made an order that in all the dioceses of his province, every young man among the faithful of more than 15 years of age was to take an oath of Peace, and join the militia of the diocese to punish those who infringed the rules of Peace. The clergy were to take the lead. This was the origin of the Paciares, a regular militia organised to make the decisions of the Associations of Peace be observed, if necessary, by force. This was,

[1] E. Lavisse, *Histoire de France*, t. II., 2nd Part, by A. Luchaire, p. 135.

indeed, the beginning of making war upon war. In certain districts, like le Quercy, a special fund was opened for the defence of Peace, the Common of the Peace, as it was called ; it was maintained by taxes called pazagiems.

With these organisations can be compared brotherhoods like the *Encapuchonné's* (the Hooded), founded by Guillaume Durand of Le Puy whose purpose was to impose peace by force upon disturbers of it. The brothers wore on their necks a leaden Statue of the Blessed Virgin with the inscription : " *Agnus Dei, qui tollis peccata mundi, da nobis pacem.*" It exercised its powers in Auvergne, Berry, Aquitaine, and Gascogne.

The benefits of a general peace would have been guaranteed to the whole of Western Europe from the end of the last quarter of the eleventh century were it not for the untimely death of the Pope and of the Emperor. In 1023 the Sovereigns of Germania and of France, Henry II. and Robert the Pious had, with this aim in view, met at Mouzon, and had arranged to meet again at the Council of Pavia, at which Pope Benedict VIII. was to preside. But in 1024 both the Head of the Church and the Head of the Empire died. Robert the Pious, who was very desirous of General Peace, had to be content with promoting the Synods, which, from one end to the other of his States, promoted the local associations for Peace. He succeeded, anyhow, in this project. "Rarely was an assembly of the nobles or of the bishops held without peace being proclaimed at it. Robbery and private wars became more rare : a new era opened for the weak and for the Peasantry." [1]

2. The " Truce of God."

The Peace of God was a means of remedying the evil of war. The Truce of God, which set a limit to the number of days on which war could be waged, was another. The founding of these institutions goes back to the Council of Elne in the Roussillon (1027). Their original idea being the strict observance of the Sabbath, the bishops, members of the Assembly, decided that from the ninth hour on Saturday until the first hour on Monday it was prohibited to attack an enemy. In 1041 the number of days on which it was forbidden to fight were considerably increased: the abbot of Cluny, the Archbishop of Arles,

[1] Paster, *Etudes sur le règne de Robert le Pieux*, page 176.

the Bishops of Avignon and Nice, recommended to the bishops of Italy a four days armistice, from Wednesday evening till Monday morning. The Bishops of Burgundy assembled in Council at Montriond in the diocese of Lausanne, in the same year, forbade any fighting, not only four days a week, but from Advent until after the Epiphany, from Septuagesima until the first Sunday after Easter, that is, during fifteen weeks of the year. The following year the Duke of Normandy added three weeks, from the Rogations to the octave of Pentecost. In 1054 The Council of Narbonne extended still more the list of days on which men at arms must remain inactive. These were, feasts of the Blessed Virgin, of Saint John the Baptist, the Apostles, Saint Justin and Saint Pastor, Saint Lawrence, Saint Michael, and vigils, and the September quarter tense.

Thus upon the initiative of the bishops assisted by princes, who were inspired by the Christian spirit of Justice and Charity, measures were taken, in the very foundations of Feudal Society, to banish the plague of war.

The Holy See lost no time in giving them its sanction. Though Benedict VIII. did not

live to preside, in Pavia, at the Proclamation
of General Peace, John XIX., in 1030,
confirmed the Peace Pact concluded between
the towns of Corbie and Amiens. It was the
Truce of God which Pope Leo IX. ratified
when he decided (probably at the Council of
Reims in 1049) that the days of dedication of
churches, and the eves of these days, were
to be days of truce. One of his successors,
Nicholas II., ordered that the Peace and
Truce of God were to be faithfully observed.
Any person failing to do so would be
anathematised. A legate of Pope Alexander
II., Cardinal Hugues, presided in 1068 at
the Council of Gerona which established the
Truce of God in Spain. The Peace of God
was introduced into Italy by the Councils
of Melzi (1089), and Troja (1093).

The whole Church was included in the
Peace and Truce of God, in the famous
Council of Clermont in 1096, when Pope
Urban II. preached the Crusade. The Canon
stipulated that monks, clergy, and women
were to enjoy from day to day the benefits
of the Peace of God, and the peasantry and
merchants were to enjoy them for three years,
owing to the high cost of food ; the property
of those going to the Crusade was to be under

the protection of the Peace of God until their return. As for war, among those who were not thus protected, it was only allowed three days a week, and again exception must be made for the weeks of Advent, and Lent. Anyone guilty of violating the Truce of God would be punished. Many times these decisions were recalled and confirmed in the Councils presided over by the Popes, whether private Councils like those in Rome in 1102 or in Reims 1119, or General Councils like the Lateran Councils in 1139 and in 1179. Gregory IX. incorporated them in the *Corpus juris canonici* in the thirteenth century.

3. *Chivalry and the Military Orders.*

In order to lessen the evils of war, the Church made still further efforts to regulate the mode of living of those who took part in it. She undertook to educate men-at-arms and to inspire them with the necessary sentiments of Justice and Charity. With this end in view, she transformed Chivalry, an institution which was military in its origin, and whose former brutal customs still survived, into a kind of militia, whose duty was to protect the weak and defend right. Gradually her intervention came to be seen in the ceremonies at which knights were created. Her ministers blessed the standard (*vexillum*), and the sword of the aspirant. A vigil and a Mass preceded the dubbing, and the essential rite which consisted in the presentation of the sword by another knight. Eventually a priest took the place of the knight and handed the sword. Thus the ceremonial which was originally of a lay character became religious. In the prayers which were recited the duties imposed upon the knight were stated : " to be the defender of churches, widows, orphans, and all those who love God, against the cruelty of heretics and pagans." " Peace be with you," said the Bishop, when giving the kiss of peace to the knight ; and having touched him thrice with the flat of the sword, he added :— " Be a brave and faithful soldier, a defender of Peace, and devoted to God." And to God was offered this prayer in which it was specified to what extent force might be used : " Oh God, you only permitted the use of the sword here below for the repression of the evil deeds of the wicked, and for the defence of justice. Grant, therefore, that your newly created knight may never use this blade to hurt anybody unjustly, but that he may use it always to defend what is just and right."

At the very time when Chivalry was undergoing this change, some religious military orders were created and organised. The Crusades gave rise to them. Lords joined together and submitted to a religious rule, to fight the Infidel and defend Christian States. In 1113 began in this form the Order of the Hospitallers, and in 1118 the Templars. Saint Bernard of Clairvaux, who was a friend of Peace, did not hesitate to give his approval to these institutions. Certainly he proscribed wars of conquest or of aggression. " That is an unworthy struggle, he wrote, whose motive is a guilty desire for greater power or territory. Military glory is not to be judged by the difficulty of campaigns, but by the justice of the cause which is defended. If your cause is not just, if your intention is not pure, you incur disgrace, rather than honour." But Bernard does not hesitate to approve of war when it is just. " It is not without reason that the Knight of Christ carries a sword. He is the minister of God for the punishment of the wicked, and the exaltation of the just. When he kills an evildoer he is not a homicide, and we must acknowledge him as an avenger in the Service of Christ, and a defender of Christian people." Upon religious soldiers the Cistercian monk imposes a rule which is inspired by the one he himself follows ; he subjects them to the three vows, poverty, chastity, obedience. Several other orders were founded subsequently with the Hospitallers and the Templars as their model. It came to pass, in the course of time that some of their members forgot the primary idea of their foundation ; considerations of gain and of conquest triumphed over those of the defence of Christian civilisation, and the pursuit of right and justice. This was not the fault of the Church, but of those who were unfaithful to their vocation.

4. *The Third Order of Saint Francis.*

In the thirteenth century the Peace and Truce of God became less indispensable in certain countries like France, where the royal power, now stronger, was better qualified to maintain order. The tendency was for the King's Peace to take the place of the Peace of the Church. But there were other countries, such as Italy, in which war continued in an endemic state. It was then

that through the efforts of Saint Francis of
Assisi new observances calculated to maintain Peace were inaugurated. The law of
mutual charity, of which the Patriarch Saint
Francis of Assisi reminds his disciples, is
incorporated in the rules of the " Third
Order," which forbade the carrying of arms
or the taking of oaths, except in certain
serious cases, such as for the restoration of
Peace. To forbid the taking of oaths in a
social organisation in which the lords
demanded an oath, the military service of
their vassals, who were, therefore, obliged
to accompany them to wars, which were
often unjust, was really causing a revolution
in Society. The church did not hesitate to
sanction it. When in 1221 the Tertiaries of
Faenza refused to accompany their lords to
the war, Pope Honorius III. approved their
action. A few years later it was the Brothers
of Penance in Italy that Pope Gregory IX.
released from their oath, which would have
obliged them to fight in the armies of their
lords. In this manner, the Franciscan ideas
brought about at least partial disarmament
in the Italian republics which were ever
ready for fighting : they prepared the way
for more peaceful times.

Thus in a social order and at a time when everything gave place to force, institutions and observances designed to protect the weak against the violence of the strong, and to maintain peace, became more and more numerous. The Peace activities of the Church assumed innumerable forms. It might be said in the words of M. Luchaire " that in attempting to describe them one is helping to point out how much indebted to the Church, in this respect, are all impartial minds who have interested themselves at any period in the moral and material progress of the human race." [1]

5. *Catholic Doctrine on War and Peace.*

By her inspiration and by her activities still more than by her institutions, the Church contributed very considerably towards the fostering of Peace among Christian peoples. Though she did not actually forbid all wars, and she could not do so, because, in accordance with tradition, she acknowledged that there were just wars, she fixed definitely the conditions in which war was permissible. She established, one might say, the law of war. Saint Thomas Aquinas,

[1] *Revue Historique,* tome XLIX, p. 404.

the illustrious contemporary of Saint Louis, was the most authentic interpreter of her doctrine. The teaching was that war is lawful only if it is just, and it can only be this, when declared by public authority, by the *prince*; so that all private wars were prohibited. It must also be in a just cause, and waged with a pure intention, such as helping the good and repressing the wicked. The belligerent was a kind of redresser of wrongs, whose duty it was to punish an enemy, considered as a guilty person. His powers were limited. There were dishonourable ruses which were prohibited, for instance practising deception by affirming to be true what was false, in order to break a promise; though it was permitted to seize property belonging to the enemy, it was forbidden to do so with covetous intentions. The virtue of justice, therefore, governed the law of war.

None the less, the Church looked upon war as an evil. From her Founder she had received as a sacred trust the gospel of peace preached in the Sermon on the Mount. . . . . Blessed are the meek, for they shall possess the land. . . . . Blessed are those that hunger and thirst after justice, for they shall be filled. . . . . Blessed are the peacemakers for

8

they shall be called the children of God.
These maxims and many similar ones inspired
the doctrine which the Church never ceased
to teach to her faithful.   In their name he
imposed upon all the strict obligations of
fulfilling their duties of justice, and of overcoming their sinful passions and covetous
desires : she preached the law of love which
ordains that we are to forget injustice,
forgive injuries, and make peace with our
enemies.   Gradually the work of salutary
teaching and the edifying example of those
who ordered their lives most faithfully
according to the law of Christ, and of the
Saints, contributed towards calming hatreds
and lessening covetousness and love of gain.
Hence many sources of discord and causes of
war disappeared.   Between nations subjected
to the law of the Gospel, it was consequently
more easy to make peace and concord prevail.

CHAPTER IV

THE WORK OF THE POPES FOR PEACE IN THE MIDDLE AGES

FROM the time when, thanks to the Popes of the eleventh century, who made many reforms, the Holy See acquired greater prestige, breaking away gradually from the grasp of secular power, and undertaking the reform of abuses which had crept into the church, it used its influence openly, in the name of its Supreme Authority, and of its Apostolic Ministry with princes, kings and emperors. It induced them to band themselves together, to make common cause against what was threatening Christian civilisation, and it prevailed upon them to put an end to the dissensions which were dividing them, and to the wars which were wasting their resources.

1. *The Holy Wars.*

There were wars which the Church did not hesitate to encourage, nor even to stir up : holy wars, or crusades whose object

was to defend the members of the great
Christian family against enemies who wished
to seize their property, make attempts on
their lives, or attacks on their faith.   At
the end of the eleventh century, when the
Turks, under the Seldjoucide dynasty, had
seized Palestine, and had begun to invade
Asia Minor, Christians were no longer safe.
Those in the East who could offer but a weak
resistance lived in daily dread of being
overrun by the destroyer. They were the first
to be attacked.   Then came the turn of
Western Christians. Pilgrimages to the Holy
Places which had been able to continue even
after the Arabian Conquest, became impossible
from the moment that the Turks came to
Jerusalem. To have allowed the Seljoucides
to pursue their Conquests, and obtain possession of the Eastern Empire, would have meant
that soon all Western Christians would have
been at their mercy.   It was, therefore,
absolutely necessary to form an alliance
of all Christian forces against them, to
organise the Holy War, the crusade, if
Europe was to be saved.

   To protect Christendom against Turkish
barbarity, and get back from their possession
the tomb of Christ, Urban II. responded to

the appeal made by the Emperor of Byzantium. The popes who had promulgated the Peace and Truce of God at the Council of Clermont, exhorted the Christians of the West at the same assembly to go to the help of their brothers in the East, and to form an alliance against Islam. This pontiff who worked so meritoriously for the cause of Peace set going the movement which succeeded after many set backs in averting the Turkish peril from Europe, though it it did not achieve the final deliverance of the tomb of Christ.

The struggle against the infidel was the sole aim of the crusade. Consequently it was necessary that the Christian forces should not be deterred from it, and that there should be no agreement come to with the Musulmans. In 1202 the Venetians prevailed upon the Crusaders to undertake the siege of Lara in Dalmatia which belonged to the Emperor of Byzantium ; Innocent III. pronounced excommunication against them, and he aimed his censure at the Crusaders themselves. When it happened, moreover, that a sovereign like Frederick II., who had set out for the Crusade, concluded Treaties of Peace with the Sultan, and purchased, at such a price, the right of entry into Jerusalem, he was condemned by Pope Gregory IX.; he was guilty of making a compact with the Infidel. The Holy City was, therefore, placed under an interdict when the emperor entered it: the churches were bare, the Altars stripped of their ornaments: no priest dared to say Mass in his presence.

Whilst from the end of the eleventh century, to the end of the thirteenth, and even the fourteenth century, Crusaders, coming from France, Germany, England, Scotland, Ireland, Sweden, and Norway, broke the onslaught of the Turks in the East, the Christians of the Iberian peninsula stopped the efforts of the Moors, who were as great a menace to Christian civilisation. Here again it was a Holy War which the Sovereigns of the Kingdoms of Spain conducted with valour, supported and encouraged by the heads of the Church.

A time came when it was not only the infidels, but heretics, the Albigenses, who threatened society by their subversive principles about the family, marriage, and property. When the Church had exhausted all peaceful means, she had recourse to force, and stirred up a Holy War against them. The social order had to be protected.

Thus it was that Pope Innocent III., having failed with all peaceful overtures, finally decided upon a Crusade against the Albigenses. When these heretics had committed crimes against peoples' rights, by murdering his legate, he exhorted all the faithful for the remission of their sins to fight courageously against the ravages of heresy, and to defend by force of arms the Christian people. This crusade was destined, unfortunately, to lose before long its religious character. The Head of the Church did all in his power, however, to preserve it, and to prevent it from degenerating into a war of conquest.

The popes of the fifteenth century were urged by the same anxieties when they organised armed expeditions against the Hussites. The Head of the Church need not have interfered in Bohemia at that time, if the rising had been merely a quite legitimate revolt of the Czech National Sentiment against Germanism, and the oppression of a foreign country. Unfortunately the disciples of John Hus, as well as defending the National claims of their master, upheld religious doctrines directly opposed to

Catholic dogma and the Christian social
order.   Because their doctrine threatened
both of these, the Holy War was preached
against its supporters.

2. *Arbitration and Pontifical Mediation.*

Whilst they were mobilising the forces of
Christendom against those who were threatening Civilisation and the Social order, the
heads of the Church were endeavouring to
avert all wars between Christian princes.
In his capacity of Suzerain of Poland, the
Two Sicilies, the Kingdom of Spain, Denmark,
the duchy of Bohemia, the kingdoms of
England, of Kiew, Dalmatia, Croatia, and
Portugal, the Pope had the right to intervene
in quarrels arising among these States ; he
exercised his right fully.   But as head of the
great Christian family, as minister of the
God of Peace, who imposes duties of justice
and charity on His faithful, the Sovereign
Pontiff acted as mediator again among all
Christian belligerents, and compelled them
to lay down their arms.

From the end of the tenth century, in
990-991, a papal legate negotiated peace
between Ethelred, the Anglo-Saxon King,
and Duke Richard of Normandy.   William

the chronicler of Malmesbury, wrote : " The
Holy See cannot permit two Christian
Princes to draw the sword against each
other." In order to put down and condemn
violence, Pope Gregory VII. claimed for the
Head of the Church an authority superior
to that of temporal princes. Acting as
judge of sovereigns such as Philip I., King
of France, and Henry IV., King of Germania,
he condemned their acts of plunder at the
same time as he denounced their attacks
upon the liberty of the Church. The great
Pope of the beginning of the thirteenth
century, Innocent III., threatened with
censure and the interdict Kings of France
and England, to compel them to make a
truce ; and when Philip-Augustus broke the
truce, the Pontiff, acting upon his authority
as representative of God, made them lay
down their arms. " We are obliged," declared
Innocent, " not only to preach peace to the
sons of peace on whom, as the Gospel says,
peace is founded, we are, in addition, obliged
to strive for peace and make it prevail." [1]
Pointing out very clearly the limits of his
right of intervention, he said on another
occasion, " We have no intention of inter-

[1] Migne, *Patrologie latine*, tome CCXV., col. 65.

vening in questions of sovereignty (which
concerns the King) unless owing to some
special privilege or some contrary custom,
these be a departure from common law ;
but we do mean to concern ourselves about
sin, the condemnation of which is undoubtedly within our province, and we mean
to exercise that right of censure against all
without distinction of persons. The royal
dignity should not take offence when asked
to accept the judgment of the Apostolic
See. The sentence pronounced against those
who will not receive messages of peace or
who refuse to listen to them must be of the
most severe kind.[1]

The tradition of Gregory VII., and
Innocent III., was continued during the
Middle Ages. In the fourteenth century,
John XXII., the first Pope who made
Avignon his ordinary residence, replied to
the King of France who questioned his right
to impose certain truces on the vassals of the
crown : "Assuredly, my son, if you give
careful consideration to the events which the
future may have in store you cannot dis-
approve of, nor find detrimental to you or
your kingdom, the exercise of the authority

[1] Migne, *Patrologie latine*, tome CCXV., col. 326.

which belongs to the Apostolic See to impose truces." In the fifteenth century when the Pope ordered the Princes to make truces, so as to band themselves together against the Turks, he threatened with excommunication those who disobeyed. Nicholas V. wrote : " In order that nothing on the part of Christians may impede the holy undertaking, the Pope wishes and commands, by virtue of the authority which he holds from the Most High, that the Christian People be at peace. The prelates and dignitaries of the Church are authorised to intervene so as to quell disturbances and spread the love of peace ; all must, at least, consent to an armistice and observe it faithfully. Those who disobey will be punished with excommunication, if individuals, and with an interdict if whole communities." In 1461 Pius II. announced his intention :—" of imposing upon all Christians an armistice of five years under penalty of excommunication." In 1470 when Venice, Florence, Naples and Milan were at war, Pope Paul II. solemnly exhorted them to lay down their arms within thirty days.

Not wishing always to exercise their authority and impose peace, the Roman

Pontiffs unceasingly pleaded its cause with belligerents, during the Middle Ages, and intervened between them, either as arbiters or as mediators, to induce them to lay down arms. To write the history of these interventions it would be necessary to write the diplomatic history of this whole period. Let us simply recall as an example, that in the conflict between France and England called The Hundred Years War, the Heads of the Church never tired of preaching peace, bringing about reconciliations and restoring friendships. Their representatives went without respite from one camp to another, bringing proposals for agreement. It was certainly no fault of theirs that these struggles which exhausted the States concerned were not ended much sooner. At the very outset of the conflict when the first clashes of arms had already occurred, John XXII. undertook to bring about a reconciliation between the kings of France and England. Benedict XII., who succeeded him, worked for it, in his turn. In 1336 he invited the sovereigns to take into consideration " the advantages of peace and harmony and the dangers of dissension, which causes the destruction of property, loss of life, and the endangering of souls, which is still more to be deplored." Reconciliation, he repeated, is necessary for the salvation of the souls of kings and of their subjects, redeemed by the blood of Jesus Christ." During ten years he exhausted himself with all these efforts for peace. Though he did not succeed in ending the quarrels between sovereigns and nations, at least he succeeded in having postponed for ten years the final outbreak of a fratricidal struggle which was to be long and bloody. The Popes who came after him continued his work for peace, and tried to bring about armistices and treaties.

The Popes of Avignon were able to live in the heart of France, and in close relations of friendship with the " Most Christian Kings " ; they realised their duties as Head of the Christian World, in spite of what was said to the contrary ; they took care to hold the balance equally between the belligerents, and they defended with equal zeal, in all the courts, the interests of peace.

The papacy did not succeed, in spite of all its efforts, in warding off war ; it took a leading part in bringing it to an end. From Rome where Pope Martin,

emerging from the great schism, held undis-
puted authority, legates set out on several occasions to exhort to peace the kings of France
and England, and the Duke of Burgundy,
Philip the Good, who being powerful, became,
for a time, the arbiter of the situation.
When, after the death of Joan of Arc at the
stake in Rouen, Philip the Good became
more amenable to ideas of peace, the pious
Cardinal Albergati undertook to bring about
a reconciliation between him and the King
of France. His attempt was crowned with
success at the Treaty of Arras in 1435. It
announced the end of the war with England.

One of the arguments that the Roman
Pontiffs made most frequent use of to keep
the peace between them was the necessity of
remaining united against Islam. This was no
traditional commonplace of diplomacy.
Although the Christians had been compelled
at the end of the thirteenth century to
evacuate Palestine entirely, the faithful
continued to contemplate a crusade. How
could it be otherwise, when gradually the
Turk was invading Asia Minor and conquering
it ?   In the fifteenth century he overran
Europe, and from all sides he was battering
down the Byzantine Empire.   The fall of

Constantinople on the 29th May, 1453, broke
down the last resistance, and with the roads
of Europe open to them the Musulmans
spread themselves over the whole Balkan
Peninsula : they ascended the valley of the
Danube, of the Save, and of the Drave ;
even the coasts of Italy were threatened.
More than ever Christian civilization was in
danger. To maintain peace among Catholic
Princes, so as to band them together against
the common enemy, was one of the constant
aims of Pontifical diplomacy, during the
Middle Ages which were drawing to a close.

CHAPTER V

MODERN TIMES

1. *From the Renascence to the Treaties of Westphalia.*

THE Renascence which marks out the beginning of what is called Modern Times had been inaugurated when the news of the fall of Constantinople came to cast a gloom over its dawning. Already the tendencies were becoming manifest which were about to urge nations, as well as individuals, to seek exclusively their own interests while caring less and less for the general interests of the great Christian family. National self-interest seemed about to override everything. The religious revolt of Protestantism, which broke out in the sixteenth century, finally sundered the bonds of mutual fellowship, which, during the Middle Ages, had bound together Christian States. In 1525 an astonishing event happened. The King of France signed a treaty of alliance with the Ottoman Ruler.

Faithful to their traditions and duties as Head of the Christian people, and common

Father of the faithful, the Popes still continued to preach union to the sovereigns of Europe, and compelled them to join together against the Turks. It was Nicholas V. who exhorted them to end their quarrels. A congress was convened at which the various Italian principalities had to come to terms ; a general peace was signed at Lodi in 1454, a peace followed by a truce was made for twenty-five years. Pius II. was exhausted by illness and infirmity, but he was none the less the indefatigable apostle of peace : his legates worked to foster peace in Italy. All the princes were invited to send their representatives to the General Congress of Mantua to settle their differences. Innocent VIII. announced to the King of Poland that he was sending to all the Courts of Europe legates entrusted with the duty of settling disputes, and of working to unite nations in a crusade to be undertaken by them all. And it is true that Pontifical diplomats negotiated treaties of peace between the Emperor Maximilian and Charles VIII., King of France.

With the discovery of America by Christopher Columbus in 1492, new causes of war arose : Portugal, which considered

9

it had established its right to own all hitherto
undiscovered countries, contested Spain's
claim to the New World. Pope Alexander VI.
averted the war which was about to break out
by giving his decision as arbiter, at the
request of the Sovereigns of Spain. With
the plenary powers of his Apostolic authority
he " gave " to Spain, on condition that
Catholicism should be propagated there, the
exclusive ownership of the countries discovered, or which would yet be discovered,
by Christopher Columbus, provided they
were not already in the possession of a
Christian power ; an imaginary boundary
marking the possessions of both countries,
was traced by the Pontiff (acts of 3rd and
4th May, 1493). By this decision the Pope
merely fixed the boundaries of what is called
to-day the Spheres of Influence of Nations
at war. His decisions made an important
contribution to the maintenance of peace
between Spain and Portugal : they were
instrumental in obtaining a peaceful solution
to the numerous frontier disputes which
arose later.

Is it a fact that this intervention of the
Pope resulted in the authorisation of colonial
wars, as well as the excesses of which their

instigators, especially the Conquistadores of the sixteenth century, made themselves guilty ? By no means. As Francis of Vittoria, the Spanish theologian of the sixteenth century, explained : the Pope was able to grant to the Spaniards the exclusive right to preach in the Indies : this was within his province since it was his right and his duty to see that the faith was propagated ; but he could not dispose of the actual territory of America in favour of the Spaniards. "The Pope can intervene in temporal questions as Spiritual Sovereign, and in Spiritual interests, but he has not this right with regard to the Indians or other infidels who are not subject to such jurisdiction." [1] In his pronouncement of 1493, Alexander VI. had only in view the Christian nations which were at war ; in 1497, in a concession made to the Portuguese, he distinctly protected the rights of the natives ; he said : "unless the inhabitants should voluntarily submit."

It can be shown still more clearly that the Papacy and the Church were in no way responsible for the atrocities which the Indians suffered at the hands of the Spaniards and Portuguese. These atrocities were not only

[1] G. Goyau, *L'Eglise Catholique et le droit des gens*, p. 56.

condemned by apostles such as Las Casas, father of the Indians, who made a public protest to the Spanish authorities, and by theologians like Francis Vittoria, who prohibited them on moral grounds : the Popes forbade them absolutely. Pope Paul III. made his pronouncement on the subject, when in 1537 he said of the Indians : " Although they are ignorant of the faith of Jesus Christ, they must not for this reason be deprived of their liberty or reduced to slavery ; but it is by preaching the gospel, and by the example of a virtuous life that they must be enticed and urged to receive the faith. They are men like us. Like all other nations who have not yet been baptised, they must enjoy their liberty, and the peaceful possession of their property ; no one has any right to molest them or cause them anxiety, about what they have received from the liberal hand of God, Lord and Father of all men."

Pontiffs like Alexander VI., and Julius II., influenced by a certain trend of the renascence which was not entirely in accordance with Christianity, may have allowed themselves to be drawn into secular ways. But in spite of everything, anxiety for the general interests of Christendom remained uppermost in their thoughts, and on more than one occasion they returned to a sense of their duty ; they then gave an edifying example by working for the restoration of peace. The Council of Lateran, which assembled in 1512, at the command of Julius II., remained faithful to tradition when it affirmed in the face of the world that "nothing is more harmful, nothing more disastrous to the Christian Republic than war."

In the sixteenth century, and during the first half of the seventeenth, one of the most important causes of conflict and wars was religious dissension, and the rivalry between France and the House of Austria. These struggles, from being at first, "wars of magnificence," undertaken by France against the Hapsburgs, became, according to the celebrated expression of Albert Sorel, "just common wars," that is, wars to break loose from the grasp of ambitious neighbours, and to make one's own life safe. The necessity of safeguarding their independence, and of guaranteeing its liberty to Italy, sometimes drew the Roman Pontiffs into the conflict, and forced them into either camp. This was, on the whole, exceptional. The majority of the Heads of the Church made a point

of remaining neutral. In the course of this
long and painful struggle almost all of them
were able, like Marcellus II., to declare their
determination to be neither French nor
Spanish, and to be nothing but the apostles of
peace, the common fathers of all the faithful.

The Roman Pontiffs pleaded for the restoration of Peace between the rivals on the
grounds of the menace of heresy and the
necessity of holding a council to remedy the
evils of protestantism, and to stamp out
abuses in the Church. The time had passed
when they could intervene as arbiters between
enemies as their predecessors had done in the
Middle Ages. The attacks upon the Pontifical
Authority by the Protestant Reformation,
the jealousies of sovereigns anxious to
establish beyond question what they considered to be their rights, prevented the
Heads of the Roman Church from acting
as judges in their quarrels. Though Leo X.
did this to a certain extent in 1518, with a
view to the crusade, and claimed the pre-
cedent of Innocent III., he was scarcely
listened to. It sometimes happened that one
side or the other requested arbitration from
the Pope, but the request was not made in
deference to his supreme authority, but to

involve him indirectly in the struggle. What lay within the Pontiffs' power, and they did not fail to do this, was to offer their mediation, and to work for the reconciliation of the parties, and to induce them to discuss the terms of a treaty through the intermediary of Apostolic Nuncios. This was what Paul III. did in the sixteenth century, and he did not hesitate to undertake the journey to Nice in 1538 to persuade Francis I. and Charles V. to become reconciled, and conclude a peace which was to last ten years. In this way one of the great Popes of the seventeenth century, Urban VIII., spared no efforts to avert the war which was impending between France and the Hapsburgs. He insisted upon the more important interests of the Christian Republic when speaking to princes who had in view nothing but their private interests. As Common Father of all he opposed the renewal of fratricidal strife. His entire diplomacy aimed at the assembling of a congress at which the terms for restoration of peace would be discussed.

It is to him that all honour is due for having, even before the war had broken out, prepared the meetings of diplomats from which emanated the famous treaties of Westphalia.

While the Roman Pontiffs were working
to maintain peace, the theologians were
defending it, for their part, by specially
defining the right of war. Two Spaniards
especially distinguished themselves by their
work : the Dominican Francis of Vittoria
(1480-1566), and the Jesuit Francis Suarez
(1548-1617). They continued and developed
the teaching of Saint Augustine and Saint
Thomas Aquinas ; they would not admit
any war to be legitimate except a just war,
that is a war in which the prince acts as a
judge, condemning and punishing the guilty
person. It was the prince's duty to decide
whether the war was just or not. However,
as he might be deceived by self-interest,
Vittoria imposed upon him the obligation
of asking the opinion of men of honour
and judgment, who would be bound to give
their opinion. In the event even of their
not being consulted, they were obliged to
do so. It was an appeal to the caution and
judgment of public opinion that the
Dominican theologian was demanding. Suarez
did not consider this sufficient. He demanded a higher authority than the
princes in conflict to decide the right
of war ; in Christian States the Pope

would act, not by virtue of direct power, but by the indirect power conferred on him by his spiritual authority. Thus he expounded the theory of Pontifical intervention in quarrels between Catholic princes, a theory, which, unfortunately, had no chance of being accepted by sovereigns who were most ambitious to be independent. It bore some fruit nevertheless, because it was instrumental in the setting up of a superior tribunal which was to settle quarrels between nations. Suarez did not foresee this result at all; it was embodied nevertheless in the logic of the principles which he had laid down.

2. *From the Treaties of Westphalia to the beginning of the nineteenth century.*

At Münster in 1648, the papacy, through the intermediary of its Nuncio, had protested against the clauses of a treaty which had secularised bishoprics and abbeys, and recognised the legal right of the religion of the princes only. By ignoring these protests, political Europe had signified to the Heads of the Church that they must take no further part in international affairs. Indeed it soon seemed that the representative of Christian right would have no option but to submit,

confronted, as he was, by nations which
had become more and more ambitious of
their autonomy, setting up armed barriers
on their frontiers, and recognising no other
law than a skilful balance of power established
by the strong at the expense of the weak.
He did not, however, surrender easily. The
Pontiffs of the second half of the seventeenth
century were not content with showing their
constant interest in peace by getting medals
struck to commemorate the great treaties.
Not disheartened by the fact that they got
little hearing, they continued their efforts
to put an end to wars. The numerous
documents preserved in the Vatican Archives
on the records of the Nunciature of Peace
(*Nunziatura della Pace*) testify to their
activities. Innocent XI. distinguished himself
particularly : he wished at all costs to restore
peace in Europe, in order to unite Christian
princes against the Turk. The victory won
by John Sobieski under the walls of Vienna,
in 1683, which brought about the liberation
of Hungary, was obtained by a certain
amount of united action, thanks to the efforts
of the Pontiff. This success was unfortunately
not followed up. No doubt there were still
thinkers like Leibnitz, and he was not a

Catholic, who regretted that the Head of the Catholic Church no longer presided as Vicar of Jesus Christ at the Assembly of Christian Nations, to impose peace upon them, but the diplomats and statesmen excluded him from their Councils and deliberations.

In the latter part of the eighteenth century the papacy was a helpless witness of the partition of Poland.

At all events the Roman Pontiffs remained faithful to their programme of peace. They made a point of living in peace with princes. Rather than break with their traditions, they prepared to lose even their States and to risk the worst misfortunes to themselves. This was the case of Pius VII., who was to see his States invaded and confiscated, and who was taken prisoner because he rejected the command of the Emperor Napoleon to extend the continental blockade to the Pontifical State, and to close its ports to the English. At all costs he wished to remain at peace with all Powers. Could there have been a greater sacrifice to the idea of peace at a time when the whole of Europe was under arms, and acknowledged only the law of force, at a time when the Pope's only defence was his weakness ?

CHAPTER VI

THE ACTIVITIES OF THE PAPACY IN THE NINETEENTH AND TWENTIETH CENTURY

In the nineteenth century, more than ever, it was force that governed relations between nations. It was the main principle of the balance of power which governed the marking out of boundaries of States at the Congress of Vienna in 1815, without having any regard for the wishes of nations. It compelled all sovereigns to arm, in order to be in a position to resist the ambitions of their neighbours. The Catholic Church was none the less persistent in its teachings that the observance of laws must be the basis of peace. On the very eve of the day that the Head of the Church, Pius IX., suffered violence, and was dispossessed of his States, he received a petition from forty bishops who complained of the burden of taxation imposed upon various countries by military necessities. The bishops stated : " The spirit of irreligion, and the disregard of law, in so-called international affairs, clear the way, in every case, for the beginning of unjust and illegal wars, or rather horrible massacres which continue to spread on all sides. The church only, therefore, can put a stop to such misfortunes." On the 10th March, 1870, while the Council of the Vatican was being held, Armenian Bishops asked Pius IX. to intervene at the Assembly "to have the law of nations solemnly proclaimed; to have the tyrannical principles of the right of the strongest expressly condemned; to have the real meaning of the divine precept, 'Thou Shalt not Kill,' announced to all; to point out once more that unjust wars are really murder and plunder; to promulgate by the infallible authority of this oecumenical Council, the conditions of a just war according to the rules of canonical law, which is everywhere trodden under foot." The war of 1870, which broke out during all this, showed only too clearly the urgent necessity of such a conciliar decision. That event, unfortunately, made it impossible to discuss the question. The Council of the Vatican had to suspend its deliberations now that the struggle had begun. Anyhow the whole affair had been submitted to the fathers; there was nothing more to be done.

Deprived of its temporal power after the taking of Rome, it seemed as though the Holy See would be reduced to playing a very minor part in international politics. The reverse happened; recalled by the widespread misery of the day it found itself reinstated in a position which it had not occupied for some time. In 1885 two great European powers, Spain and Germany, asked Pope Leo XIII. to arbitrate in a quarrel which had arisen between them with regard to the Caroline Islands. The decision was given with such judgment that not only did it give full satisfaction to the parties, but it ensured for the Roman Pontiff the greatest prestige. When in 1898 Tsar Nicholas II. convened the States at the Hague with a view to considering the problems of disarmament, and peaceful solutions of quarrels, his minister asked Leo XIII. to give the support of all his spiritual authority to the great work of confirming peace. The Pope replied, through the intermediary of his Secretary of State, Cardinal Rampolla, by denouncing the cause of the widespread disorder in international society; the fundamental rules of justice and right were entirely set aside for expediency and the needs of the balance of power.

" The institution of mediation and arbitration seems to be the most suitable remedy for so disastrous a state of affairs. It is in accordance in all respects with the desires of the Holy See." It was no fault of the Pope that his contribution to the work of peace-making was not greater. The mistrust of a great European sovereign prevented this ; in this way the Conferences for peace were denied a collaboration which would have helped towards their success.

When difficulties arose in South America ; when a war was on the point of breaking out, about 1900, between Chili and the Argentine Republic, bishops of both countries intervened ; they aroused a general feeling which induced the governments of both countries to have recourse to the arbitration of the King of England. Peace was secured. A colossal Statue of Christ, erected in 1904 on the Summit of the Andes, 4,000 metres above sea level, commemorates what must be considered a victory for the spirit of Christianity. " These mountains shall topple, declared the Chilian bishop Jara, who was one of the originators of peace, before Argentine and Chili shall break the peace, sworn at the feet of Christ the

Redeemer." About the same time, between Brazil, Bolivia, and Peru, a quarrel began. These States appealed to the Pope to settle it. An arbitration tribunal, presided over by the Apostolic Nuncios, was held. The decision was pronounced in the name of Pius X. The representative of the Holy See was able to express his satisfaction "for having drawn closer the bond of fraternity between two nations for whom Providence has reserved the highest destinies." He added : " The tribunal by assuring the principle of arbitration marks a new step of progress towards the goal to which humanity aspires, and helps to confirm the hope that the day is not far off when the struggle for extermination which afflicts human society will cease : trusting in arbitration for the solution of international problems there will be no more mention of strong or weak nations, and brute force will not prevail without the force of right, and at the same time the words of the psalmist, *justitia et pax osculatae sunt* will become a reality."

While they were thus actively engaged, the Roman Pontiffs kept also reminding peoples and sovereigns of the traditional teaching of the Church on International Law.

As Fathers of the great human family they sought to imbue minds with the Christian spirit of Justice and Charity ; to limit struggles for nationality, and to remind the various powers of their duties of fraternity towards each other, so as to confront, in accordance with the principles of the Gospel, the right of might, with the might of right. After the Caroline Islands arbitration, Leo XIII. remarked what noteworthy benefits the Roman pontificate would procure for the world if '' in the enjoyment of its liberty, and all its rights, it could without opposition exercise in all things its influence for the salvation of the human race.'' Three years later, in 1899, having pointed out to the Cardinals who were assembled in Consistory the frightful prospects of a European war, and denounced the expenses and dangers of an armed peace, he expounded the Christian principles of justice and charity, which make order and security prevail among nations ; principles of which the Church would remain the indefatigable apostle.

Pius X. echoed the ideas of Leo XIII., when, on the 11th June, 1911, in reply to a request for his approval of the Carnegie Foundation for International Peace, he declared that Peace, such as the Catholic Church recommends, is peace obtained by law and order, founded on the respect for love of right, and on the spirit of justice and charity. The Pontiff referred besides to the part which should be reserved for the Holy See in the peaceful settlement of international quarrels. "As Common Father of the faithful the Pope is independent of all States ; he does not uphold the private interests of any people, but he is the defender of all." On the 24th May, 1914, exactly two months before the beginning of the crisis which led to one of the most dreadful wars the world has known, the Pontiff celebrated, on the occasion of the Centenary of the Edict of Milan, the triumph of the Cross of the Saviour ; and added, that in order to prevent armed conflicts and guarantee to nations the benefits of a lasting and a fruitful peace, while face to face with disastrous wars and armaments becoming every day more deadly, it was necessary above all to foster the principles of Justice and Christian Charity in souls. "The Cross of the Saviour," said the Pope, "must appear as a symbol of Peace." The answer he made to the Ambassador of Austria, who asked him a

few weeks later in the name of his Master
to bless the Austrian troops, is well known :
" I give my blessing to Peace."

Pius X. saw only the beginning of the
catastrophe which convulsed the whole world
from 1914 to 1918. His successor witnessed
all its dreadful developments. From the
beginning of his pontificate, Benedict XV.
pointed out the deep-seated causes of war :
the disregard of Charity, contempt for
authority, class war, exaggerated desire for
luxury. He strongly urged nations to submit
to arbitration and peaceful settlement of
international quarrels instead of shedding
blood in war. By every means in his power
the Pontiff intervened to alleviate the far-
reaching consequences of the struggle, pro-
testing against the open violation of the
Christian law of war. His decisions as
mediator were so impartial and discriminating
as to earn for him more and more reverence
and respect. Was it not extraordinary, at
such a time, to see this man, unarmed, strong
only in the power and authority conferred on
him by Christ, extending words of reconciliation to adversaries who seemed to put no trust
in anything but the strength of their armies ?

The peace which the Pope wanted was a

peace founded on right, and on the just aspirations of nations. He asserted it especially in his famous declaration on 1st August, 1917, when he invited the belligerents to enter into pourparlers. In it he asked that peace might be concluded on the basis of right " making allowance, as far as was just and possible, for the lawful desires of nations, and at the same time co-ordinating private interests with the general good of Human Society." It was also a programme for the future that ne drafted, to avoid the recurrence of similar disasters, a programme that he was the first of sovereigns to prescribe with such clearness and precision. He suggested.

General and proportional reduction of armaments.

The setting up of obligatory arbitration.

The introduction of international sanctions.

When, at last, the war was over, Benedict XV. strove for a real peace, asserting that the Evangelical doctrine demanded forgiveness of injuries, even love for one's enemies, since we are all the children of one Heavenly Father, and brothers in Jesus Christ. The Roman Pontiff gave his approval to the efforts made to avert new quarrels in the future. It was to the League of Nations, established in Geneva, that he referred when he said : " All nations united in a league, founded on Christian law, would be assured of the active and earnest co-operation of the Church in all their undertakings inspired by the justice of charity."[1]

Pius XI., successor of Benedict XV., carried on the same work for these ideals. Rising above the nations, he preached to all the obligation of forgiving injuries, and of becoming reconciled with our enemies, in a spirit of Justice and Charity. He appealed to the representatives of nations assembled in Geneva to lessen all possible chances of conflict. He affirmed at the same time this truth. If there is no worldly institution competent to impose upon the ensemble of nations a general code of legislation adapted to our times, there "exists a divine institution which is in a position to safeguard the inviolability of the law of nations, an institution which belongs to all nations, and which shines forth over all nations. It possesses highest authority. It is deserving of reverence and respect by reason of the fulness of its teachings and mission : it is the Church of Christ.

[1] Encyclical *Pacem* of 23rd May, 1920.

By virtue of her nature and of her constitution, and because she has prevailed
throughout so many centuries to the edifica-
tion of so many generations, she alone seems
able to accomplish such a task. The storms
of war have not shaken her : indeed they
have increased her strength.[1] "

* * *

Faithful to her past traditions, the Catholic
Church still continues to fulfil in the world
her mission of justice and charity. The
Pope, Common Father of the great Christian
family, approves of the peaceful settlement
of all quarrels which arise between his
children : he intervenes to bring them
together. Minister of the God of Peace, he
works unceasingly to bring peace to all men
of good will, The Catholic doctrine of which
he is the guardian is so fruitful in its teachings ;
the Catholic tradition which he defends, is
so rich in experience, that her Head cannot
but realise the hopes founded on him by all
those who work to avert the menace of
renewed conflicts and shedding of blood,
and to accomplish the reign of true peace,
the peace of the God of Love.

[1] Encyclical Letter, *Ubi arcano Dei*, 23rd Dec., 1922. See *Pie
XI, et la Paix* by Mgr. Beaupin (Paris : Bloud et Gay, 1928).

PART III

ORGANISATION AND ACTIVITY OF THE LEAGUE
OF NATIONS

I

INTRODUCTORY

1. *Principle.*—The League of Nations was constituted by the Covenant which formed the first part (articles 1 to 24) of the treaties of Versailles, Saint Germain, Trianon, and Neuilly.

The purpose of the institution is to develop between the States composing it permanent relations of peaceful collaboration, and thus to reduce to a minimum the risk of conflict and of war. This programme, as may be seen, coincides precisely with the views set forth by His Holiness, Benedict XV., in his pontifical Note to the heads of belligerent states. The fundamental data of the Covenant are thus in complete harmony with the requirements of Christian morality whilst corresponding to the practical needs of the contemporary world.

The interdependence between nation and nation is even becoming more pronounced, and more complex. Political, economic, and social life is becoming more and more international. Consequently everything is liable to become a subject of dispute or of tension if the relations between states are not organised on a basis of justice and law. That is precisely the rôle that has fallen to the League of Nations—to define the law, and make justice respected.

In its present form, which is still in transition, the institution in Geneva constitutes an important stage on the way towards an organic international status; the world has got beyond the period of anarchy, and is entering on a period of organisation. Not only does the League of Nations maintain between states direct and permanent contacts, which help considerably to bring about the settlement of disputes by agreement, but besides it serves them as a valuable instrument of co-operation since it possesses organs that correspond to each class of problems and are prepared to play the part of mediator between conflicting national interests. Though its activities have hitherto been applied only to particular points, yet the work it has already accomplished is by no means negligeable. And the institution consolidates itself by the very fact of its continuance.

II

ORGANISATION OF THE LEAGUE

2. *Structure.* The League of Nations in the form laid down in the Treaties is a federal league involving for its members a twofold bond of political and judiciary alliance. The adherents to the Covenant pledge themselves on the one hand to combine their military and economic forces to the extent laid down by the Covenant itself, on the other hand not to have recourse to arms as a solution of any dispute that may arise between members, until they have exhausted all the resources afforded by peaceful methods —arbitration, judicial proceedings, commissions of enquiry, mediation. No nation parts with its independence, for the executive organs of the League can address to its members only counsels and recommendations, or, if need be, remonstrances, but not orders. In principle all decisions must be unanimous, the delegates who reach these decisions being the immediate representatives of the powers who chose them, and not agents of the League.[1]

---

[1] This rule of unanimity admits, however, of certain noteworthy exceptions, the most important of which is the admission to the League of new members by a two-thirds majority.

Ought the League of Nations to be a Superstate exercising legislative, executive, and judiciary powers over the States which are its members ? As things are at present, apart from the fact that such a conception of its rôle is quite beyond what is warranted by actual facts, it would have the serious drawback of appearing to be at variance with patriotism, and would thus neutralise the useful, if limited, efforts of the institution in Geneva. The Super State if it ever does come into being [1] must, if it is to be anything but an artificial and precarious construction, be the outcome of gradual evolution [2] whereby, owing to the economic pressure of material needs as well as to the acceptance of the idea by the leaders of opinion, the public will eventually become aware of a solidarity which they perceive but dimly to-day.

[1] To sceptics and to critics systematically hostile to the League it is well to recall the fact that in other domains history records transformations that are no less thorough, for instance the abolition of slavery which flourished for so many centuries, and without which the Ancients could not so much as conceive that Society could exist.

[2] The contention of the partisans of the Super State that the world is evolving in the direction of federalism seems to be in accordance with facts. Witness the multiplication of international associations, unions, conventions of all kinds, forming at the present day a huge network, as well as the many existing treaties from which it is already possible to deduce, as the League of Nations is endeavouring to do, the principles of a system of law common to all civilised States.

Whatever be the lines followed by the League in its further development, it will necessarily remain of its very nature a political and temporal institution. And so it is impossible to endorse the view— unfortunately widespread in Catholic circles —that the Church is the only possible league of the nations. To maintain that would be to forget the traditional and fundamental distinction, recalled by Leo XIII. in various encyclicals and notably in *Immortale Dei*, between the two societies, the spiritual and the temporal, which are to be harmonized but not confused. Positive international law, although it comes within the scope of the moral law, and in so far forth falls under the judgment of the Church, nevertheless comes within the ordinary competence of the public authorities, as well for its elaboration as for its application, this latter being, to meet eventualities, equipped with the necessary sanctions.[1]

3. *Members.* (a) Original members : forty-four States or Dominions are, of right,

---

[1] On this point see two articles by M. Louis Le Fur, Professor in the School of Law in the University of Paris : " Catholicisme et Société des Nations," and " L'Eglise et le droit des Gens " in the *Bulletin Catholique International*, Nos. 8 and 32, January, 1926, and March, 1928.

members of the League, whether *ipso facto*
as in the case of the thirty-one signatories
of the Peace Treaty,[1] including the four
dominions [2] of the British Empire and India ;
or in virtue of the declaration of adhesion
to the Covenant, within the two months
preceding its taking effect, viz., thirteen
States, neutral during the Great War, the
list of which is to be found in the Annex
of the Treaty.[3]

All of the States save three are, at present,
members of the League.[4]

(*b*) Admitted Members. The other States
are simply admitted at their request. This
request can be acceded to only in the case
of a Dominion or colony which

> 1. Governs itself freely ; 2. Gives effective
> guarantees of its sincere intention to
> fulfil its international obligations ; 3.
> Accepts the ruling of the League with
> respect to its armaments (this condition

[1] Belgium, Bolivia, Brazil, Cuba, Ecuador, France, Greece,
Guatemala, Haiti, Hedjaz, Honduras, Italy, Japan, Liberia,
Nicaragua, Panama, Peru, Poland, Portugal, Roumania, United
Kingdom, Yugoslavia, Siam, Czechoslovakia, Uruguay. China
became a member in virtue of the Treaty of Saint Germain.

[2] South Africa, Australia, Canada, New Zealand. (Ireland
had not entered the League when this was written. Trans.)

[3] Argentine, Chili, Colombia, Denmark, Spain, Norway,
Paraguay, Netherlands (Holland), Persia, Salvador, Sweden,
Switzerland, Venezuela.

[4] The three are the United States, the Hedjaz, Ecuador.

is not intended for the original members).
The League in full session votes on the
admission, a two-thirds majority sufficing.
In this way fourteen admissions have
been made.[1]

Owing to the use of the expression State,
Dominion, Colony in the Covenant, the Holy
See, described generally in international law
as a Power, cannot be included in the list
of possible members of the League. This
clause of the Covenant is not to be taken
as, on the part of those who drew it up, a
manifestation of hostility to the Holy See,
but the natural consequence of the distinction
drawn above between the two societies, the
spiritual and the temporal. The Papacy is
not, from the material point of view, prepared
to assume the majority of the obligations
incumbent on members. While from the
religious point of view it would have no
interest in intervening in many of the political
and economic questions that arise. Owing
to their complicated and contentious nature

---

[1] The First Assembly (1920) admitted Albania, Austria,
Bulgaria, Costa-Rica, Finland, Luxemburg ; the Second (1921) :
Esthonia, Latvia, Lithuania ; the Third (1922) : Hungary ;
the Fourth (1923) : Abyssinia and the Irish Free State ; the
Fifth (1924) : the Dominican Republic ; the Seventh : Germany,
(1926).

intervention on the part of the Holy See would uselessly [1] endanger the religious and moral prestige of the Vatican, and of the spiritual authority of the common Father of the faithful.[2]

Each member has the right of secession from the League on giving two years' notice of its intention, provided it has fulfilled all its international obligations.[3]

Any member may be expelled from the League for violation of any of its pledges

---

[1] The situation to-day differs profoundly from the period when the international community and Christendom were conterminous. The League of Nations includes a certain number of non-Christian States, and in the others the unity of faith is so completely broken up that a pontifical participation in decisions reached at Geneva would run great risk of exercising no influence upon their execution.

[2] Collaboration between the Church, a hierarchial spiritual society, and the temporal societies, the States composing the League is nevertheless highly desirable in certain domains where spiritual and temporal interests intermingle. This can readily be brought about through the usual diplomatic channels between particular States and the Vatican, whether permanent diplomatic relations between Rome and Geneva be set up, or whether definite questions be dealt with as they arise by means of temporary diplomatic missions. See the series of three volumes by Père Yves de la Brière, S.J., *L'Organisation internationale du monde contemporain et la Papanté souveraine*. Paris : Editions Spes. (This note was written before the signing of the Lateran Treaty which gave the Holy See a new international status. *Trans.*)

[3] Costa-Rica, Brazil, and Spain have taken advantage of this provision. The Argentine Republic, Bolivia, Peru and Honduras have not taken part in several Assemblies. Spain decided, before the two years notice had expired, to resume her place at Geneva on the invitation of the Council of the League to reconsider the decision to withdraw.

arising out of the Covenant. This expulsion must be voted unanimously.[1]

4. *The Assembly*.—The Assembly is composed of the representatives of the States members of the League. Each State or Dominion has one vote, and chooses three delegates, who are accompanied by substitutes, experts, and secretaries. It meets regularly once a year on the first Monday in September in Geneva.[2] If the circumstances seem to call for it, the Council may decide by a majority vote to convene an extraordinary meeting.

The Assembly appoints six Committees, on which each of the States members of the League is represented. They deal respectively with :—

(*a*) Constitutional and judicial questions.

(*b*) Technical Organisation.

[1] The Union of Soviet Socialist Republics which considers itself as a sort of League of proletarian nations, Turkey, Mexico, and Egypt, have not yet applied for admission to the League. (The new political party just formed in Egypt has adopted admission to the League as one of the " planks " of its " platform." Ed.)

[2] On this occasion an annual religious service is held, usually on the second Sunday in September in the Church of Notre Dame at Geneva. With the Bishop of the diocese presiding, and in presence of the Catholic delegates of the Assembly, and members of the Secretariate, a preacher dwells on the great Christian principles of international justice and charity, and prayers are offered up for the success of the Session. At about the same time the Protestants hold a service in the Church of St. Peter.

(*d*) Finance.

(*e*) Various questions.

(*f*) Political questions.

Besides these, sub-committees are set up by the President on the proposal of the Secretariate, and with the approval of the main Committee concerned.

The Assembly conducts its proceedings in public. It comes to no decision on any point until the Report of the Committee competent on the particular question has been received and distributed. The agenda includes a discussion of the Report of the Council (presented by the Secretary General) on its work since the last meeting of the Assembly ; on the work of the Secretariate and the steps taken to carry out the decisions of the Assembly. Next comes discussion of questions held over from preceding Assemblies, or brought forward either by the Council or by some member.

The powers of the Assembly fall under three heads :—

(1) *Powers peculiar to itself.*

(*a*) The voting of the League's budget and

(*b*) The admission of new members.

(*c*) The election to the Council of non-permanent members.

(*d*) Fresh enquiry into situations threatening world peace.

(*e*) The regulation of its own procedure.

(2) *Powers held jointly with the Council.*

(*a*) Revision of the Covenant.

(*b*) Nomination of the Judges of the Permanent Court at the Hague, and of the Secretary General of the League.

(3) *Powers held alternately with the Council.*

All other questions, apart from those reserved to the Council, belong indifferently to either body. Contrary to what is sometimes supposed, the relations between the Council and the Assembly do not resemble the relations between public bodies in the various constitutional arrangements. Here there is question of two diplomatic bodies possessing powers now peculiar to one or the other, now joint, and again alternate. In this last case, which is the commonest, the body which first takes cognizance of a given question follows it up until it has been threshed out, abandoned, or held over.

5. *Council.*—At the outset the Council consisted of four permanent seats,[1] and four

---

[1] The British Empire, France, Japan, and Italy.

non-permanent. To-day it is made up of
five permanent, and nine non-permanent
seats. The Council has power to increase the
number of seats, designating the new holder
or holders with the approval of a majority of
the Assembly. Thus Germany on her entry
into the League received, thanks to the
working of this procedure, a permanent seat
on the Council. The Council can likewise
increase the number of non-permanent seats
with the approval of a majority of the
Assembly, but the designation of the holders
falls to the Assembly.[1]

The inequality among the State members
that arises out of their representation or
non representation on the Council is considerably diminished by the fact that any
State may be called upon to send representatives when the question under consideration is of peculiar interest to it.

When the Council acts as mediator (Art. 15)
the parties to the dispute are not counted
in the voting on the decision, which must be
unanimous like all the other decisions of the
Council or of the Assembly, whenever the
Covenant does not specify otherwise.

[1] The present (1931-2) holders of the non-permanent seats
on the Council are: Spain, China, Panama, Poland, Yugo-
Slavia, Venezuela, Guatemala, Irish Free State, Norway.

The powers of the Council are as follows :—

(*a*) The carrying out of the Peace Treaties (the administration of Dantzig and of the Sarre Valley, the control of disarmament, the prolongation of economic measures, the protection of minorities, etc.)

(*b*) The regulation of internal procedure.

(*c*) The question of the transfer of the seat of the League.

(*d*) Disarmament (the drawing up of the scheme, the nomination of the permanent military commission, the regulation of private manufactures of arms, the authorisation to exceed the limits laid down, etc.)

(*e*) The maintenance of peace (measures for preventing aggressive acts, and the danger of them, the carrying out of a sentence of arbitration that is not being executed, the examination of disputes that have not been submitted to arbitration).

(*f*) Sanctions (military measures in case of collective action by the League, expulsion of violaters of the Covenant).

(*g*) Mandates (the consideration of the Reports submitted by the mandatory powers and by the Commission of Mandates).

6. *Court of Justice.*—Unlike the Assembly and the Council, the Permanent Court of

International Justice was not set up by the
Covenant, but only forecasted. Its creation
in 1920-22 was the work of two statutory
organs basing themselves on the labours of
a committee of jurists which met at the
Hague, the future seat of the Court, in the
summer of 1920.

The judges to the number of fifteen, four
of whom are substitutes, are elected for nine
years from a panel of candidates[1] put
forward by the "national group" of the
Permanent Court of Arbitration at the
Hague.[2] They must at the same time obtain
a majority of votes in the Council and the
Assembly.   It is recommended that the
principal forms of civilisation, and the various
juridical systems be borne in mind when the
choice of judges is being made.   Each party
to a dispute has a right to a judge of its
nationality in the Court so that the
impartiality of the Court's decisions may be

[1] Four candidates, only two of whom may be of its own
nationality, may be put forward by each State.
[2] In virtue of the Hague Conventions 1899 and 1907, each
power is entitled to four judges to act as arbitrators, these four
forming its "national group" at the Permanent Court of
Arbitration at The Hague. Despite its pompous name the latter
is merely a list of possible arbitrators. This is kept by a
permanent office which is administered by a Council formed of
the representatives at The Hague of the signatories of the
agreements of 1907.

guaranteed and so that national susceptibilities may not be disregarded in the drawing up of its findings.

The Court of International Justice may give consultations on legal points referred to it by the Council or the Assembly.

It passes judgment on disputes submitted to it whether voluntarily by the parties concerned or compulsorily in a certain number of cases laid down by international conventions.

7. *The Secretariat.*—Though ranking below the Assembly, the Council, and the Court, the Secretariat nevertheless constitutes a most important organisation owing to its permanence, its function as a collector and source of information, and the valuable part it plays as regards registration, liaison, preparation, co-ordination, and even initiative.

The employees of the League of Nations form a little corps of international civil servants, headed by a Secretary General nominated unanimously by the Council, and by a majority vote in the Assembly [1] ; the Secretary General in his turn chooses his

[1] The first Secretary General, Sir Eric Drummond, is named in Annexe II. of the Covenant. The Deputy Secretary General is a Frenchman, M. Avenol, the three Under-Secretaries-General are M. Dufour Féronce, a German ; Count Paulucci di Calboli, an Italian ; and M. Sugimura, a Japanese.

collaborators. However, appointments, conditions of service, and the financial administration of the Secretariat are strictly supervised by the Assembly.

The international Civil Service established at Geneva is divided into about a dozen sections :—

The Political Section.

The Economic and Financial Section.

The Transit Section.

The Administrative Commissions (Saar and Dantzig), and Minorities Section.

The Disarmament Section.

The Health Section.

The Social Section.

The Intellectual Co-operation and International Bureaux Section.

The Legal Section.

The Information Section.

8. *The Auxiliary Organisations.* The League of Nations has at its disposal a certain number of auxiliary organisations controlled by the Assembly and the Council, and working in close touch with the Secretariat, but enjoying a more or less full measure of independence so that even States which are not members may utilise them. Though each of these auxiliary organisations

has features of its own, all of them fall under one or other of three heads—autonomous organisations, technical bodies, and consultative committees.

A. *Autonomous organisations* — (*a*) The International Labour Organisation, which owes its origin to clause xiii. of the Treaty of Versailles, but is closely linked up with the League of Nations as regards financial administration and exchange of mutual services.

(*b*) Intellectual Co-operation.—As early as its first Assembly the League has shown itself anxious to promote co-operation in the sphere of thought by facilitating the exchange of intellectual services, and the intercommunication of the results of scientific investigation. In 1921 a committee of twelve members, most of them well-known savants (the philosopher Bergson, the scientist Madame Curie, the physicist Einstein, etc.) was appointed by the Council. At the close of 1924, thanks to the generosity of the French government, Intellectual Co-operation was endowed with an Institute which was founded in Paris in the buildings of the Palais Royal. This Institute, though situated in Paris, remains none the less a strictly

international foundation. Its task is to call
forth, encourage, and co-ordinate initiatives
of all kinds in the domain of science and of
education.

The organisation of this intellectual co-
operation comprises an Executive Committee
of five members (in addition to the original
Committee enlarged), and the Institute itself
divided into six sections : Literary Relations,
Artistic Relations, Legal Affairs, Scientific
Relations, University Relations, Information.

B. *Technical Organisations.*—These resemble the autonomous bodies. They do not,
however, constitute such complete units, and
in their functioning they depend directly on
certain services of the Secretariat.

The two organisations for Transit and for
Health have been definitely formed : they
each comprise a general Conference, a consultative Commission, and a Secretariat,
which is really the corresponding section of
the general Secretariat of the League.

On the other hand the economic and
financial organisation is still without a
definitive framework. Besides the provisional
organisation which still continues, the
Eighth Assembly has set up a consultative
Committee whose duty it is to follow up the

recommendations of the Conference of Geneva held in 1927.

C. *Advisory Committees*.

The permanent committees set up by the Covenant are the Advisory Committee for military, naval, and air questions, and the Committee of Mandates.

In addition to these the Council has appointed a large number of temporary committees, such as the Advisory Committee for the Protection of Childhood and Youth with a special sub-committee of experts to enquire into the traffic in women and children ; the Advisory Committee on Opium ; the Committee of Experts for the codification of international law ; the Preparatory Commission on Disarmament, etc., etc.

III

ACTIVITIES OF THE LEAGUE OF NATIONS

9. *International Organisation*. — The Covenant came into operation on the 10th January, 1920. The Council met for the first time on the 16th of the same month, and the Assembly held its first Session from the 15th November to the 18th December in the same year. As was to be expected

the first period was devoted to the task of internal organisation. It was a huge and difficult task. The Covenant was quite a brief and hastily drawn up document, and there was entire lack of precedents. Moreover, for reasons contradictory in themselves, but all converging to the same result, the victorious, the neutral, and the defeated States all regarded with equal mistrust the beginnings of the new institution in Geneva. In the eight years that have gone by since then, that institution has developed, completed, and strengthened itself in a methodical and continuous manner, thereby proving to any impartial observer the emptiness of certain apprehensions, and the trifling character of certain criticisms.

10. *Political Action.*—The political action of the League has been directed mainly to fixing frontiers left undetermined by the Peace Treaty, and to preventing or stopping armed conflicts which threatened the peace of the world.

(*a*) *Frontiers.* The League settled in 1920 the question of the Aland Islands which were claimed by Sweden and Finland ; carried out the partition of Upper Silesia claimed by Poland and Germany (1921) ; defined the frontier between Albania and Yugoslavia (1922) ; settled the disputes between Poland and Czechoslovakia over the district of Javorzina (1923) ; decided the possession of Memel which was in dispute between Lithuania and the Allies (1924).

On the other hand the League did not succeed in securing acceptance for its solution of the question of Vilna (1920-3) ; nor of that of Mosul (1924-5). But, at least, its intervention prevented these quarrels from developing into armed conflicts, and prepared the way for an ultimate settlement.

(b) *Armed conflicts.* The League was appealed to in the case of the Italo-Greek incident in August, 1923, and of the Bulgaro-Greek incident of October, 1925. In the former case the mediation of the Council which was appealed to by Greece, in accordance with Clauses 12 and 15 of the Covenant, could not be exercised, the Conference of Ambassadors, on which the victims of the incident had called, being competent to deal with the question : but the Council collaborated with the Conference in effecting a settlement. On the other hand the second intervention following on serious frontier incidents in Macedonia, affords a typical

instance of effective mediation on the part
of the Council, and of the rapid carrying out
of clauses 10, 11, and 12 of the Covenant.

11. *Economic and financial action.* The
League has exerted itself to facilitate international communications (Barcelona Conference, 1921), to simplify customs regulations
(Geneva Conference, 1923). It has held
enquiries on the subject of double income
tax, tax evasions, dishonest commercial
transactions, false coinage, etc., etc. The
theoretical studies of the experts and
employees of the League, and the Conferences
that it has got together (*e.g.* the Financial
Conference at Brussels in 1920) are regarded
everywhere as authoritative, and have been
more or less directly availed of by the various
States. In particular they led to the Dawes
plan and various monetary reforms.

The League was directly responsible for
the financial reconstruction of certain States
which had been ruined by the War.

(*a*) Financial disasters had brought Austria
to an all but desperate political, social, and
economic situation, when the League took
cognizance of the matter (15 August, 1922).
In two months a Committee of the Council,
and the financial department of the League,

worked out a plan of reconstruction. It was no sooner put into operation than it brought about an immediate stabilisation of the rate of exchange. Four months later the deposits in the banks had increased fourfold, and credit dealings, both home and foreign, had once more become possible. At the end of six months it had become possible to balance the budget. In 1925 Austria, having carried out its financial reforms, was freed from the financial control of the League.

(b) Hungary, finding itself in a position which, though less serious than that of Austria, was nevertheless critical, appealed to the League in 1923. The re-establishment of credit, the balancing of the budget, and financial reform, were successfully carried out in what was, on the whole, a very brief space of time.

In May, 1927, on the initiative of France, the League summoned an international economic conference in which fifty countries took part. It studied the economic difficulties prevailing at the present time in industry, commerce, and agriculture, together with the means of overcoming them. As an outcome of its labours, there were drafted in November, 1927, a convention for the abolition of prohibitions on exports and imports. It is the first plurilateral treaty of commerce, and marks an important stage in the international organisation of commerce.[1]

12. *Humanitarian Activities.*—The Covenant assigns to the League of Nations a preponderating rôle in the struggle against the scourges that afflict mankind, and which being of their nature international, can be combated only by a concerted international effort.

This activity has taken the form of the drafting and the signature of conventions aiming at the total but gradual suppression of the traffic in opium, at the putting down of the traffic in women and in obscene literature, and at the protection of children.[2]

In matters of Health the League acts as a clearing house for information concerning epidemics, and for demographic statistics ; it is working for the standardisation of serums and biological products ; it sends missions

[1] Greece and Esthonia likewise benefited by the assistance of the League in their effort to attain to a more healthy financial position.

[2] This moral and charitable aspect of League of Nations activities was certain to engage the attention of Catholics in a very particular way. Their participation in the struggle against the survivals of slavery, the traffic in women, and in drugs, took effect through the Catholic Union of International Studies. This organisation supplied to the Secretariat of the League and to its advisory committees ample documents and statistics on these matters.

to the centres of epidemics, and to organise public health work in various countries, notably in South American States and China.

Further, the League has devoted itself to relieving the last remaining victims of the European War, and of the war in the Near East. Nearly half a million prisoners, most of whom had been kept in Siberia, or had got lost there, were repatriated under the direction of Dr. Nansen, High Commissioner of the League of Nations. He also directed the relief work for Greek, Armenian, and Russian refugees. After the defeat of the Greek Armies in Asia Minor there took place an exodus *en masse* of the Greek population of Ionia to the number of more than 750,000. At the request of the Government of Athens the League undertook the settlement of the refugees. The task was immensely complicated by the Greco-Turk exchange of population decided upon by the Treaty of Lausanne, and by the reciprocal emigration of Greeks and Bulgars. Extensive districts in Macedonia, hitherto half desert, were peopled by more than a million emigrants. The financial organisation at Geneva guaranteed the issue of the necessary loans.

13. *Social Action.* Social action is the

peculiar province of the International Labour Organisation. There has been created a remarkable world centre of information which conducts enquiries, collects and keeps up-to-date facts and statistics of all kinds bearing on labour and social conditions. It has forwarded to the various governments nearly forty recommendations or draft conventions, and has registered some 200 ratifications.

IV

THE LEAGUE OF NATIONS AND THE MAINTENANCE OF PEACE

14. *Preventive Action.*—The rôle of the League is, not so much to find a way out of quarrels that have reached an acute stage, still less those that have actually resulted in hostilities, as to prevent disputes, by organising such close collaboration between nations as to bring about gradually and naturally the effective internationalisation of a certain number of public services.

The technical organisations of the League, which utilize or strengthen the bonds of solidarity already in existence, are gradually substituting a real federation of associated peoples for what was formerly a mere mosaic

of States. In this way they work in the cause
of peace just as efficaciously as the institutions
expressly intended for smoothing over difficulties and deciding disputes. The League is
following on much the same lines as national
governments, which succeeded in main-
taining permanent peace and security within
their frontiers, only when they had attained
the full administrative and constitutional development of the machinery of government.

15. *Settlement of Disputes.*—From the outset the League imposes on its members, in
case of conflict, the obligatory recourse to
some peaceful means of settlement, but it
leaves them free in their choice of those
means. In case of the breakdown of diplomatic
negociations they may have recourse either to
arbitration, or to a judicial sentence, or to the
mediation of the Council or of the Assembly.[1]

[1] In current speech " arbitration " is often taken in a broad
sense as equivalent to " peaceful solution " whether by
arbitration properly so called or by mediation, enquiry, or
sentence. This is likewise, we think, the meaning adopted in
the various pontifical documents dealing with arbitration, in
particular in the letter from Cardinal Rampolla, acting in the
name of Leo XIII., to the Tsar of Russia at the time of the
Hague Conference. The Pope asked that the principle and
the practices of arbitration should be the object of " unanimous
acceptance and assent," and deplored the absence of " a
system of legal and moral methods calculated to assure the
rights of each." In the absence of such methods, he continued,
" there was no other option than to have recourse to arms.
Hence the emulation between States in the development of
their military power." (February 10th, 1899).

(*a*) Arbitration may be sought either from arbitrators chosen by the parties, or designated by the Treaty, or else from the Hague Court of Arbitration, established in 1907, and subsisting concurrently with the Court of International Justice.

Arbitration is recommended by the Covenant in such cases as the interpretation of a treaty, the determination of a point of international law, the reality of a fact alleged as constituting a breach of an international undertaking, the extent and nature of the reparations due for such a breach.

(*b*) Judicial decisions are the province of the Permanent Court of International Justice set up by the League of Nations. Its intervention is compulsory in certain cases, viz., for the States which have accepted what is known as the facultative clause ; for States which have previously acknowledged, in an arbitration treaty signed by them, the competence of this court : for the special cases specified by treaties and conventions ; for difficulties arising out of the regulation of international communications, out of the international organisation of Labour, out of the exercises of colonial mandates, and finally out of the status of minorities.

An amendment to the Covenant names as susceptible of settlement by judicial sentence the disputes for which a settlement by arbitration is recommended. It is an undoubted fact that the Court of International Justice, owing to its personnel, and to its permanence, offers very decided advantages as compared with other arbitral bodies, and that in point of fact it will be preferred to them.

(c) The Mediation of the Council may be sought in all cases in which the competence of the Court of International Justice is not compulsory. In practice it must be sought for all non-justiciable cases, that is to say, those in which the political aspect is more pronounced than the legal.

The Assembly may be appealed to in the case of a dispute whether by a member or by the Council. In that case it enjoys the prerogatives of the latter. It is obvious that mediations by the Assembly must necessarily be infrequent.

16. *Recourse to arms.* Recourse to arms is forbidden :—

(a) Before the putting into operation of one of the three above-named pacific measures (first moratorium of hostilities).

(b) Before the lapse of a period of three months counting from the date on which sentence is pronounced or the report of the Council handed in (second moratorium).

(c) In any case recourse to arms is forbidden against the plaintiff State which accepts the sentence—the unanimous report of the Council being equivalent to a sentence, —or against the defendant State which carries it out in good faith.

War is permissible after the lapse of a period of nine months (six months for the Council to present its report, plus three months for reflection) in case the Council fails to secure unanimity, account not being taken of the disputants.

Sanctions or punitive measures may be taken when a State violates the provisions of the Covenant. They consist principally in an international blockade isolating diplomatically, economically, and financially, the member that has violated the Covenant. It is calculated that this measure of coercion, though less violent than war, will none the less reduce the recalcitrant power to submission. Military measures are regarded as being rather of a complementary nature.

The members of the League are free to

take part in these sanctions or not, as they think best. This liberty undoubtedly constitutes one of the weak points of the system organised by the League for the maintenance of Peace. The Protocol of Geneva (2nd October, 1924) which attempted to define and determine precisely the obligations arising out of the Covenant, and to fill up certain lacunae in it, was supported by France, but could not be carried out owing to the hostility of the British Empire and Dominions, Japan, Italy, Scandinavia, the Netherlands, and the majority of the Latin American States.

Nevertheless the efforts put forth for the working out of the Protocol have not been barren of results. Its spirit animated the Treaties of Locarno in 1925. Moreover, the debates at the Eighth Assembly in 1927, with its outlawry of war passed on the motion of Poland, indicate a return to favour of the principles of the Protocol, the final destiny of which is not yet determined.

Far from devoting itself to a Utopian or barren task, the League of Nations is, at bottom, merely responding to the desire of His Holiness, Benedict XV., who in his note of the 1st August, 1917, asks that measures should be concerted and sanctions determined upon against the State that should refuse either to submit international questions to arbitration, or to accept its decisions. Besides there is a striking parallelism between the peace efforts of Geneva, and the programme put by the Sovereign Pontiff before governments of good will, viz., substitution of the moral force of law for the material force of arms : agreement on the simultaneous and reciprocal reduction of armaments, retaining only what is necessary and sufficient for the maintenance of public order : the institution of arbitration with its lofty functions.

17. *Reduction of armaments.* The reduction of armaments is the logical consequence of recourse to pacific processes of settlement, but it is also a prerequisite condition of such recourse, for without disarmament States might be tempted anew to have recourse to violent means, or, at least, to offer prolonged resistance to international sanctions.

In seeking a solution the League has been oscillating between two formulas—security first (the French point of view), and disarmament first (the English point of view). The former of the two at present tends to carry the day, and the solution of the problem of disarmament, properly so called, is thereby postponed. The close and continuous study of this problem was undertaken, since the foundation of the League, first by the permanent advisory Committee, then by a temporary mixed Committee, finally by the Committee Preparatory to the Conference on Disarmament. All that this last has succeeded in doing up to the present is to determine the points (not very numerous) on which there is a probability of an immediate agreement, and the others (more important) which must be reserved for future consideration. It has not yet been possible to fix a date for the meeting of the Conference itself.[1]

[1] This momentous Conference is actually sitting at the moment of writing, February 9th, 1932.

PART IV

THE INTERNATIONAL LABOUR ORGANISATION

CHAPTER I

REASONS FOR ITS CREATION

1. THE necessity for legislation protecting the worker against the evils of excessive competition in modern large-scale industries, called for some international organisation to legislate. As long as such protective legislation did not exist, labour conditions, not only for adult men, but still more for women and children, might be very harmful. In many cases employers themselves called for legislation. In point of fact all industrialised countries have to some extent or other passed legislation of this kind.

2. But this legislation, at least, for a period of some years, threatened to over-burden with overhead charges the industries of the countries that had adopted it, and as a result to place them in an unfavourable position in foreign markets.

3. In order, therefore, that international trade competition should not work out to the disadvantage of the countries having the

best labour conditions, it was necessary that this protective legislation should, as far as possible, be uniform throughout the various countries, and this could be brought about only by international agreement.

CHAPTER II

HISTORICAL PRECEDENTS

1. ACTION taken by various governments. This idea of an international agreement is by no means new : as far back as 1876 it led to action on the part of the Swiss government. The latter took up again the attempt in 1890. At the request of the Kaiser Wilhelm II., a conference took place at Berlin. But nothing positive came of it.

2. The International Association for the legal protection of workers was founded in Paris in 1900 in the course of a congress called together on the occasion of the Universal Exhibition in that city. The membership of this Association is drawn from a variety of sources. There are specialists in labour legislation, University professors, government officials, representatives of the Labour Movement, industrial magnates. The Holy See was represented at it.

The Association brought together at Berne in 1905 an international technical conference which drafted three conventions, the first dealing with unemployment, the second with the night employment of women, the third with certain noxious properties of phosphorous as used in the manufacture of matches. The following year a diplomatic conference held in the same city ratified the work of the previous conference. The two conventions dealing, respectively, with the night labour of women, and with phosphorus, had received, on the eve of the war of 1914-1918, the ratification of a considerable number of governments.

In 1913 another technical conference met at Berne to study the question of the hours of work of women employed in industry, and that of the prohibition of the night employment of children.

3. On several occasions during the course of the War expression had been given to the idea that the Peace Settlement ought to include some provision for labour legislation, and ought to initiate a scheme of international action which should allow of its being realised in the best conditions.

A considerable number of trades union congresses had passed resolutions to this effect, not only such as had met in one or

other of the allied countries, but also in
the central empires, and in neutral countries,
not only congresses of a socialistic tendency,
but also those under Catholic auspices.

The Peace Treaties, of which the Treaty
of Versailles (28th June, 1919) is the proto-
type, were to go far to meet these resolutions.

CHAPTER III

THE TREATY OF VERSAILLES. PRINCIPLES

THE thirteenth Section of this Treaty (Clauses 387-427) was devoted to Labour. It sets up an international labour organisation within the framework of the League of Nations, and lays down a certain number of principles, the adoption of which is essential to the maintenance of world peace.

For with a clear sightedness, which deserves to be emphasized, the authors of the Treaty affirm that peace between States can be real and lasting only if within each State social peace between class and class is maintained. But there can be no social peace that is not founded on the basis of social justice. And so the authors of the Treaty agreed that there should be laid down certain principles which might be regarded, in the present state of the world, as the essentials of that social justice, and such as were calculated to assure to the working classes labour conditions that are really humane.

These principles are not defined in a
dogmatic manner, nor put forward as a
complete and definitive charter of labour.
Rather are they set forth as results of
experience acquired in most of the great
industrial countries. It is expressly recognized that " differences of climate, of
manners and customs, of economic oppor-
tunity, and industrial tradition," make it
difficult to attain absolute uniformity of
labour conditions.

These principles are embodied in the nine
propositions reproduced below. It will be
interesting to compare them with those laid
down by Pope Leo XIII. in his encyclical
of the 15th May, 1891, on the Condition of
the Working Classes.

The Dignity of the Worker.

The first principle, referred to as a " direc-
tive principle," takes a very general form.
It is thus expressed in clause 427 of the Treaty
of Versailles :—

" . . . . labour ought not to be considered
merely as a chattel or as an article of
commerce."

By which we must understand that in
dealing with the conditions of labour we

must not lose sight of the fact that in reality we are speaking of the worker, and that the worker is a man.

On several occasions Leo XIII. had stressed his disapproval of those who " dishonour in them (the workers) human nature by unworthy and degrading conditions," and of " speculators who, making no distinction between man and machine, overwork their employees to an unlimited extent."

" It is right," he said elsewhere, " that they should respect in him (the worker) the dignity of a man raised still higher by the dignity of the Christian."

It will, doubtless, be considered that the Pontiff's text is notably clearer than the still somewhat timid and hesitating formula of the Treaty. But it is impossible not to recognise the close kinship of thought between the two.

The Right of Association.

The second principle of the Treaty lays down " the right of association for all purposes not at variance with the laws, and that for employees no less than for employers."

Leo XIII. had already insisted at length on how much may be expected, for the solution of the questions with which he is dealing, from professional associations, guilds, and trades unions, with regard to which he lays it down that " the right to existence has been conferred on them by nature itself."

Wages.

" The payment to workers of wages which will secure to them a standard of living such as is understood in their times and in their respective countries to be right and proper " . . . is that not a sort of echo of an admirable passage of the encyclical in which Leo XIII. lays down the conditions which wages ought to fulfil ? He concludes it with this formula that " wages ought not to be insufficient to support a sober and honest workingman." It is, with a very slight difference in the expression, on both sides the same proclamation of the right of the working man to live on the product of his labour.

The Pope says again :—

" Justice demands that the State should have a care for its workers. It ought to see to it that they receive their due share of the goods which they procure for the community . . . . "

The Duration of Work.

If we consider next with the Treaty the question of the Eight Hours Day or the Forty Eight Hours Week put forward as " an aim to be attained wherever it has not already been attained," we are unable to extract from the Encyclical, for purposes of comparison, any such precise figures.

It is because the Pontifical document is dealing with the matter from the doctrinal point of view. But it does not fail to protest against those who " imperil the health of the workers by excessive work," and to lay down the principle " that the duration of rest ought to be measured by the outlay of energy which needs to be restored."

And elsewhere :

" . . . . Thus the number of hours in the day's work ought not to exceed the limits of the workers' strength, and the intervals of rest ought to be proportioned to the nature of the work and to the health of the worker, and should be regulated according to circumstances of time and place. The worker who digs out of the earth what is most deeply hidden in it, stone, iron, and copper, undergoes a labour such that short duration should compensate for fatigue and for damage to

health. It is also just that the seasons of the
year should be taken into consideration.
Certain work may be light at one season,
and at another unbearable, or, at least,
very hard."

Sunday Rest.

" The right to daily rest as well as the
cessation of work on the Lord's Day ought
to be an express or tacit condition in every
contract between employer and employed.
When that condition is not present the
contract is not a moral one, for nobody may
require or permit the violation of the duties
of man towards God and towards himself."
(Leo XIII.)

The Treaty on its side stipulates " the
adoption of a weekly holiday of twenty-four
hours, which should include Sunday whenever
possible."

Child Labour.

The Treaty calls for " the suppression of
child labour, and the obligation of setting
such limits to the labour of young people
of both sexes as may permit of their con-
tinuing their education and safeguarding
their physical development."

In the Encyclical we find the same preoccupation supported by the same motives.

" What an able-bodied man can accomplish in the heyday of his powers cannot be justly demanded of a woman or a child. Children in particular—and this needs to be strictly observed—ought not to enter the factory until they reach the age at which their physical, intellectual, and moral powers are sufficiently developed."

The three last principles laid down in the Treaty do not lend themselves so easily to textual comparison with the Encyclical, but it suffices to read them to see that they are in the same line of thought, and are merely a practical adaptation to particular situations of the general rules set forth in the Encyclical.

" The principle of equal wages, without distinction of sex, for equal work."

"The labour regulations obtaining in each country should be such as to guarantee equitable economic treatment to all workers residing legally in the country."

"Each State should organise a corps of inspectors, which should include women, so as to secure the enforcement of the laws and regulations for the protection of the workers."

The parallel just instituted between the teachings of Leo XIII.'s Encyclical and the principles set forth in the Treaty of Versailles possesses an apologetic value which deserves to be brought out. The Pope in 1891, when labour legislation was still in its infancy, was far from having before his eyes the results of experience which the authors of the Treaty of Versailles had at their disposal. He nevertheless deduces from the Christian moral law applications which human wisdom and experience were to approve of twenty years later, and to set forth in almost the same terms. Truly a telling answer to those who maintain that the Church, whatever services she may have rendered in the past, is incapable of meeting the wants of the peoples of to-day. On the contrary she continues to be the light of contemporary society, and gives to it, even in difficult and thorny questions, the teachings that are best adapted to their needs, and the most practical and useful guidance.

CHAPTER IV

ORGANISATIONS CREATED BY THE TREATY OF VERSAILLES

To carry out the application of the principles just set forth, the Treaty makes provision for a labour organisation built up on a plan similar to that of the League of Nations.

The framework of this Organisation is made up of an annual conference, an administrative council, and an international labour bureau.

The members of the international organisation are in the first place the States Members of the League. But a provision was made from the outset that States which had not signed the Covenant, can take part in this permanent labour organisation. This was, for instance, the case with Austria and Germany which were admitted into the organisation in November, 1919, though Austria was to enter the League only in 1922, Germany not till 1926.

1. *The International Conference.*

The conference which meets annually is made up of the representatives of the states members of the organisation at the rate of four to each state. Of these two are delegates of the government, one a delegate of the employers, the fourth a delegate of the workers. The government of each country nominates all four representatives. One rule is laid down, viz., that the delegate of the employer and that of the workers shall be chosen in conjunction with the most representative of their respective organisations. This wide formula leaves to the governments a sufficiently great power of initiative, while securing the representation at the Conference both of economic interests and those of class.

Each of the delegates votes individually. For most of the divisions, in particular those that result in draft conventions or in recommendations, a two-thirds majority of the votes cast is required.

The deliberations of the Conference follow an agenda which has been previously submitted to the various governments. A questionnaire on each of the points liable to result in a decision is sent to them often more than a year before the date of the session. The replies of the governments are collected, analysed, and classified in a report drawn up by the International Bureau of Labour.

This report, copies of which are sent to all the members of the Organisation several months before the Assembly, is discussed in Committee, and in public session, along with the proposals which the Bureau may think well to formulate in accordance with the replies received.

The deliberations of the conference result in the voting of two classes of resolutions.

(*a*) Drafts of international conventions to be submitted for ratification by the states members of the Organisation in accordance with their respective national codes of law. Consequent on this ratification the states concerned are bound for a period of years in the same manner as by a Treaty. Provision is made for a process of adhesion to or repudiation of, the convention.

(*b*) Recommendations conceived in more general terms, and tending to suggest legislation on lines appropriate to the genius of each particular nation. This legislation they will be free to modify subsequently, as may suit them, or even to repeal altogether.

The conference is free also to pass resolutions which are merely expressions of opinion.

2. *The Administrative Council.*

The Council consists of twenty-four members, eight of whom are representatives of the principal industrial states of the world, four represent states nominated in virtue of a system of rotation, while the employers group and the workers group of the conference each elect six members. These latter twelve members have a purely international standing.

The Council meets four times a year. To it are entrusted all the problems of organisation and administration of the International Labour Office. It draws up the agenda for the annual Conferences, and supervises the carrying out of the conventions in the various countries.

3. *International Labour Office.*

The I.L.O. is the permanent and administrative body of the organisation. It has its headquarters at Geneva. Its director from

the outset has been a former French Minister
of State, M. Albert Thomas.

It is at once an organ of documentation [1]
and of action.

It compiles a scientific documentation on
all questions coming within its scope, as well
as information on all social movements,
agitations, claims, strikes, and organisations
whether of employers or employed. When
necessary it undertakes enquiries on special
problems.

Having at its disposal periodical organs
and other publications of various kinds, it
is enabled to bring out studies and documents.
In this way it translates and publishes the
principal legislative enactments in various
countries on matters concerning labour.
Special mention must be made of the
important enquiry on production which was
published in four volumes.

Facts, statistics, and other documents are
collected every year to help the international
conference in its work.

As an organ of action it keeps a close watch
on ratification, in the various countries, of

[1] This very useful French word is, I think, not as yet familiar
to non-specialist Readers. Some word in English is certainly
needed to cover a collection of facts, statistics, and documents
of various kinds bearing on a given point.

conventions and agreements that have been
come to. It keeps in touch not only with
governments, but with organisations of
employers and of workers with a view to
promote the progress of legislation, and the
amelioration of labour conditions.

CHAPTER V

THE CARRYING OUT OF THE PLAN

THE international conferences have taken place regularly each year. First at Washington (November, 1919), then at Genoa (1920), and since 1921 at Geneva. In the year 1926 two sessions were held successively, one of them being devoted, as had been that of 1920, to the conditions of labour among seagoing men.

It is not possible to enumerate all the questions which have been embodied in draft conventions. We shall call attention to the best known and most important.

The Eight-hours working day (1919).

The protection of motherhood (1919).

Prohibition of night-work of women (1919).

Prohibition of employment of children under 14 (1919).

Unemployment and the organisation of employment bureaux (1919).

Problems connected with agricultural labour —in particular the protection of women and children employed in agriculture (1921).

The laying down of general principles governing factory inspection (1923).

The utilisation of workingmen's leisure hours (1924).

Compensation for accidents (1925).

Obligatory sick insurance (1927).

Year by year a certain progress is observable, both in the efficiency of the methods of working, and in the way in which the states members of the organisation are represented at the Assembly. The number of incomplete delegations, *i.e.*, of delegations composed solely of employers and workmen's representatives is diminishing steadily. In 1929, 39 States were represented ; this figure rose from 27 in 1920 to 39 in 1921 and 1922, 42 in 1923, 40 in 1924, 46 in 1925, 39 in 1926, and 43 in 1927.

According to the report submitted by the Director to the sixth session (June, 1927) 229 ratifications of the various conventions had been made. In September, 1928, the figure stood at 256, to which must be added 33 ratifications made by the competent national authority, but not yet officially brought to the notice of the I.L.O., as well as seven conditional ratifications, making a total of 296.

CHAPTER VI

PRACTICAL RESULTS OF THE INSTITUTION.

WE must emphasize, in the first place, the inestimable value of the documentation got together by the I.L.O., and the immense services which it renders to all who have to study labour conditions and labour organisations, be they professors and students, or politicians and governments.

Then there is the progress which may be expected to result from the exchange of views which takes place every year on questions carefully prepared by competent specialists of every country.

Social progress takes on a solid and durable character when it is realized by way of international agreements, from which a Government finds it harder to break away than it does to secure the abrogation of a law. Therein lies an element of security for the workers of all countries which is highly favourable to social peace.

We must emphasize, in conclusion, the fact

that the best part of the activities of this international organisation is directed towards embodying in people's ways of thinking, in manners, and in institutions reforms which, for the most part, are simply the confirmation of the explicit requirements of Christian morality.

On several occasions, moreover, the Director of the I.L.O.[1] has, without finding his views controverted, paid a tribute to the beneficial activities of Catholics, and, in particular, has pointed out the services rendered by the Christian workingmen's organisations, the international federation of which counts some four million adherents. He has not hesitated to reject the unjustifiable claim of the Socialists who, in certain countries, arrogate to themselves as a sort of monopoly the right to speak in the name of the working classes.

NOTE.—At the end of 1931 appeared an important and authoritative work on the International Labour Office, viz. :

The International Labour Organisation. The First Decade. Preface by Albert Thomas. (London : Allen and Unwin).

[1] M. Albert Thomas.

APPENDIX.

Catholic Union of International Studies

(IRISH SECTION)

A Programme of Studies

I.—*Catholic Teaching on International Relations.*

    1. Morality and the teachings of the Gospel govern not only the relations between individuals but also the relation between Governments and between Nations.

    2. The Church approves of and blesses Christian Patriotism.

    3. The Church condemns exaggerated nationalism.

    4. The Catholic teaching admits the legitimateness of war in certain circumstances. But the Church is definitely against war.

    5. The Church desires the establishment of a real " association," " family," of nations.

    6. This association can fully succeed only if it is based on Christian law and on Christian virtues, humility, justice, and, above all, Charity.

II.—*Catholic National and International Peace Organisations.*

    a. General Historical Sketch. The Oxford Congress of 1925.

    b. Existing International Organisations :

        (1) Ika.

        (2) Pax Romana.

        (3) Caritas Internationalis Catholica.

        (4) Catholic Union of International Studies.

    c. Existing National Organisations, *e.g.* the Catholic Council for International Relations in England, the Catholic Association for International Peace in U.S.A., the League " Justice et Paix " and the " Association Populaire Chrétienne pour la Paix " in France.

III.—*Origin of the present League of Nations.*

    a. Principal historical facts. Previous tendencies or attempts in this direction.

    b. Causes leading to the League of Nations :

        (1) The expansion or development of Christian Teaching.

        (2) A perversion of the Christian Spirit, Humanitarianism, accounting for certain defects of the League of Nations.

        (3) The progress of civilisation leading to increased and multiplied international relations of all sorts, economic interdependence, unification and standardisation of civilised life, international conventions, international associations and congresses between savants, social reformers, etc., sports, athletics, scouting, freemasonry.

        (4) The Great War leading to intense desire to end war.

    c. The various influences which contributed to the drawing up of the Covenant of the League of Nations.

IV.—*The League of Nations as it appears at present.*

    a. Its Principles.

    b. Its Structure.

        (1) Fundamental Organisms : 1. The Assembly. 2. The Council, 3. The Secretariat.

        (2) Auxiliary Organisms. 1. International Labour Bureau. 2. Committee of Intellectual Co-Operation. 3. International Institute of Intellectual Co-Operation.

    c. Life of the League of Nations.

    d. Questions of Security and Disarmament.

V.—*Criticism of the League of Nations.*

    a. Its Shortcomings.

        (1) Disputable criticism, *e.g.*, that the League of Nations is an instrument of Freemasonry, or a Super-state, or an English weapon against France, or a league of big nations against the small, etc.

        (2) Nevertheless, in its present form the League of Nations deserves serious reproaches, the principal reproach being that it is exclusively lay, and that in the Covenant there is no mention of God nor of the Church. **Insufficient guarantees and sanctions.**

    (3) One may criticize the complicated nature of the Mandate system and of the machinery of the League in general.

b. Its Advantages.

    (1) *Political*, actual settlement of international disputes.

    (2) *Economic and welfare*—financial reconstruction of Austria and Hungary, work for war prisoners, migrants, hygiene, struggle against world diseases.

    (3) *Intellectual*, Committee of Intellectual Co-Operation, help to students, good understanding between the intellectual classes.

    (4) *Moral*, struggle against White Slave traffic, pornography, slavery, drug traffic.

    (5) *Social*, Work of the International Labour Bureau.

VI.—*Catholic Attitude towards the League of Nations.*

a. In general, prudent and watchful but sincere and effective sympathy.

b. Therefore conclusions :—

    (1) Let us try to correct rather than to destroy what actually exists.

    (2) Let us work at the primary task, without which exterior means of pacification would be futile, viz., the pacification of minds by prayer and the development of Christian virtues, by intellectual relations and friendly intercourse of all kinds.

Made and Printed in Ireland by Browne and Nolan, Ltd., Dublin.